HOW TO LEAD WHEN YOU'RE NOT IN CHARGE

HOW TO
LEAD
WHEN YOU'RE
NOT
IN CHARGE

LEVERAGING INFLUENCE

WHEN YOU LACK AUTHORITY

CLAY SCROGGINS

ZONDERVAN
REFLECTIVE

ZONDERVAN REFLECTIVE

How to Lead When You're Not in Charge
Copyright © 2017 by Clay Scroggins

ISBN 978-0-310-53157-9 (hardcover)

ISBN 978-0-310-53696-3 (International Trade Paper Edition)

ISBN 978-0-310-53158-6 (ebook)

ISBN 978-0-310-53160-9 (audio)

Requests for information should be addressed to:
Zondervan, 3900 *Sparks Dr. SE, Grand Rapids, Michigan 49546*

Scripture quotations are taken from the Holy Bible, New International
Version®, NIV®. Copyright © 1973, 1978, 1984, 2011 by Biblica, Inc.® Used
by permission of Zondervan. All rights reserved worldwide. www.Zondervan
.com. The "NIV" and "New International Version" are trademarks registered
in the United States Patent and Trademark Office by Biblica, Inc.®

Any internet addresses (websites, blogs, etc.) and telephone numbers in this
book are offered as a resource. They are not intended in any way to be or
imply an endorsement by Zondervan, nor does Zondervan vouch for the
content of these sites and numbers for the life of this book.

No part of this publication may be reproduced, stored in a retrieval system,
or transmitted in any form or by any means—electronic, mechanical,
photocopy, recording, or any other—except for brief quotations in printed
reviews, without the prior permission of the publisher.

Art direction: *Tammy Johnson*
Interior design: *Denise Froehlich*
Cover photo: © *Sensay/Shutterstock*

Printed in the United States of America

23 24 25 26 27 LBC 15 14 13 12 11

For those hungry to help others through leadership, this book is for you.

CONTENTS

Autonomy is a myth.

It's a myth passed from one generation of wannabe leaders to the next. Eventually, every leader is forced to come to terms with the reality that *everybody is accountable to somebody*. Like most life lessons, the sooner a leader embraces this, the better. Leaders who wrap themselves in the security blanket of "If I were in charge" or "When I'm in charge" as an excuse for poor performance and lack of initiative will most likely never be in charge. On the other hand, the real leaders in an organization will find a way to lead the charge until they are in charge. Ultimately, those are the folks great leaders put in charge.

I've been on both sides of this equation. I remember sitting in a restaurant with my leadership team the Monday after I announced to a ballroom full of folks that we were starting a new church. The six of us had worked together for several years. I smiled and said, "Congratulations, we are *they!*" You know, *they*—the folks everybody in management complains about. *We were they*. I'm not sure it had dawned on us that from that point forward we didn't really have anybody to complain about or blame.

That was twenty-two years ago. They are still *they* and they have gone the distance to build an extraordinary organization. They were prepared for the day they finally became *they*. I chose that particular team because they had led well in an organization that neither honored nor encouraged leadership. I'd watched 'em lead when they weren't in charge. So I knew they were the group to put in charge. When you find people who can get things done in an organization conspiring against them, you've found leaders.

Why?

Great leaders leverage influence and relationships over title and position. When a leader is left with nothing to leverage other than title and position, the end is near. The best leaders lead like they're not in charge even when they are. The best leaders become *the* leaders by mastering the art of leading when they're not in charge. And that's why the book you're holding in your hands will be one of the most, if not the most, pivotal leadership books you'll ever read. If you want to build a leadership culture in your organization, you should make this book required reading for everyone on your team.

I've had the privilege of working with Clay Scroggins since he was a student at Georgia Tech. Clay has been an integral part of our organization for fourteen years. He started out as an intern. When he graduated from Tech with an industrial engineering degree, we hired him to lead our student ministry. His parents probably were . . . well . . . they're happy now.

Anyway.

Clay was our student pastor when my kids were in high school. So I was paying attention. When he was twenty-five, I asked him to start filling in for me on Sundays when I was gone or taking a break. When he was the whopping age of thirty, I asked him to step into the lead pastor role of the third-largest campus in our network of churches. Now Clay serves as lead pastor of North Point Community Church—my old job.

Clay was making a difference in our organization long before he was in charge of anything significant. Everything he touched got bigger and better whether he was in charge of it or not. Several years ago, I asked him at the last minute to do the teaching at our bimonthly all-staff meeting. He chose to talk about what he had learned about leading beyond his title, position, and authority. It was amazing. I remember thinking, *I could never talk about this with any moral authority because I'm in charge.* My wife, Sandra, turned to me and said, "This needs to be a book!" I agreed but didn't mention it to Clay. Sometime later, he asked me if I thought this would be a good book topic. I said, "Absolutely."

So here it is.

This isn't theory. These principles and applications are organic. They are rooted in organizational reality. If you aren't convinced already, you will be. You don't have to be in charge to make a difference. You can lead without being in charge!

ANDY STANLEY

Writing these next few paragraphs has been my favorite part of this entire process. In Romans 16, the apostle Paul had a full-on chapter of his own acknowledgments and it just seems like a great idea for all of us. These are mine . . .

Thank you to my wife, Jenny. I still remember the first time we met. I thought you were pretty amazing then, but I had no idea. No matter where we go, I'm home with you. Thank you for allowing me the margin to write this book. You have been steadfast, loving, incredibly supportive, and in it with me from the first keystroke. It's you and me till the end! Thank you to our kids. I hope being pastor's kids offers more than it costs you.

Thank you to my parents and sisters. I had the greatest childhood I could've imagined. I just hope Jenny and I can create the same amount of love, stability, and joy you gave me. To Lee and Donna, your love for Jesus is creating a legacy that our children's kids will certainly benefit from. Thank you!

For the last two decades, our church has been a massive gift in my life. Andy and Sandra, thank you alone doesn't cut it. You have led our church with so much integrity, faithfulness, and humility. I'm in tears thinking about how much gratitude I have for both of you. And thank you to an amazingly gifted team of volunteers and staff who sacrificially lead every week. I've been trying my hardest to repay, but I'll never be able to match the gift you've been to me.

Thank you to those who were instrumental in helping me write this book:

- Ben Ortlip: You told me the key to writing was to begin the day by putting my face on the ground and begging

God to inspire me. If nothing else, you told me, it would cause the blood to rush to my head. That was fantastic advice and still makes me laugh.

- Suzy Gray and Belinda Randall: It's really difficult to work with people you don't enjoy, and this whole thing has been a blast for me because of you! You two are servant-hearted, smart, and so driven. Thank you.
- Ryan Pazdur: You've made this whole process so easy. Thank you for your patience, kindness, graciousness, and honesty.
- Justin Elam: On the morning of March 19, 2014, I was hurriedly trying to finish this talk for our all-staff meeting. You agreed to meet with me that morning and you gave me illustrations, one-liners, stories, and quotes that were so inspiring to me. I owe you a lot.
- Lane Jones: Thank you for telling me to be me when I was writing. That was huge.
- Matt Bevier: Thank you for reading a few of these chapters early on. Your words from across the world were bigger than you'll ever know.

Thank you to my bros Bryson and Brad. Most people let everyone know a few things, but we've chosen to let a few people know everything. I think it's just better that way. Thank you for being such a huge encouragement and inspiration to me.

Thank you to Megan Gross for keeping life organized and fun.

Thank you to our NPCC leadership team. Most of what I've learned about leading without authority, I've learned from each of you.

Oh, and thanks to Brad Jones. Is that what you were looking for?

PART I

Understanding
Our Challenge

CHAPTER 1

THE
ODDITY
OF
LEADERSHIP

I guess I've always wanted to be a leader.

Perhaps it started with the safety patrol in fifth grade. As if being the oldest in elementary school was not enough of an ego boost, our school selected a few of the most eager kids to serve on the team that patrolled the carpool lane. Something came over me as I put on that yellow hard hat and reflective sash. I had swagger. With just the slightest hand gesture, I could force two tons of steel to come to a complete stop. That's power.

Maybe it started when I entered the student government presidential race in tenth grade. For some odd reason, I was on this creative kick, trying to leverage popular hip-hop songs as my campaign slogans.

"Back that thing up" and vote for Clay. Thank you, Juvenile.

"Say my name, say my name" and vote for Clay. I see you, Beyoncé.

It's quite embarrassing now, but somehow it worked.

Or maybe it was when I subtly lobbied to be voted captain of the varsity baseball team. I was just good enough to make the team but not good enough to actually play. As disheartening as that was, becoming captain of the team seemed to be enough to satisfy my itch for leadership. "What happens in the dugout is more important than what happens on the field" became my stump speech.

Those were the moments I felt alive. Unfortunately, those times were few and far between. The rest of the time I was just another kid in class. When I had authority, I could lead. If I had no authority, I was just waiting my turn.

Sadly, through my high school years and beyond, I missed more opportunities than I took. I see that now when I look back on my first role in ministry as a student pastor. Our weekly event met on Sunday afternoons, but the best thing we were doing was mobilizing students to serve as small group leaders for kids during our morning services. Think about it. What would have helped you more as a student? Sitting in a class and listening to someone lecture you? Or actually leading your own group of younger kids and having to do some of the teaching yourself? The answer was as obvious then as it is now. Unfortunately, I didn't have the courage to refocus our efforts and resources to encourage *even more* students to serve. Hindsight is 20/20, but the future doesn't have to be so blurry if we wear the right glasses.

As I look back over my first few jobs, the common theme that has run through every one of them is regret. I regret the times I didn't speak up. I regret the times I twiddled my thumbs, waiting for someone to tell me what to do. I regret feeling like a victim to the structure or hierarchy of the organization.

Life teaches us that the authority to lead and the opportunity to lead are a package deal. We think they go hand in hand like cranberry sauce and turkey. When we're given the authority to lead—a title, a uniform, a corner office—then, and only then, will we have the opportunity to lead. But that's just not true.

WAITING TO BE IN CHARGE

As we wait for the authority of leadership to present itself, are we supposed to just sit on the sidelines before we can attempt anything with even a resemblance to leadership? So it seems. Growing up, my perspective was that if you were in charge, you were naturally leading something. Parents were in charge and they seemed to be leading. The principal at school was definitely in charge. She seemed to be leading. Even the bus driver who was supposedly in charge of the bus yelled at everyone like he was trying to lead. The line leader in kindergarten was in charge, at least for the day. And what was everyone else in line doing? Just waiting until it was their turn.

Do you remember how that felt in school? I remember feeling so powerless, so helpless, and so impotent. I was one of thirty kids sitting in a row with a full bladder. Yet I couldn't relinquish one drop of urine without someone with authority leading me to the bathroom. The reality is that ninety-nine percent of my childhood was me being led by someone with authority. When someone else is telling you what to do, you don't have to lead anything. You don't even have to think. You just learn to put your mind in neutral and go with the flow. When someone else is leading you, it seems as though there is no leading left to be done. So you just wait.

No one likes waiting for a turn to lead—to be the one making the decisions—but we all know what it feels like. You have ideas, but you feel like no one will listen because you don't have the microphone. You're not *leading* the meeting; you're just *in* the meeting. When you tried to share your plan last time, you felt ignored. Or even worse, you felt like you were seen as a renegade or a thorn in the side of the one in charge. So you decide that maybe you're just better off if you quit trying.

They'll never listen.

It's going to be like this forever. I'll just shut up and go with it.

They just don't get it, and there's no sense in trying.

My first real job as an adult reinforced this. Though my desk sat on the seventeenth floor in a downtown Atlanta skyscraper like the rest of my team, everyone was eager to tell me what to do because his or her altitude on the organizational chart was higher than mine. And it seemed that the higher they were positioned on the chart, the lower the requested task was. I remember thinking, *I don't mind getting your dry cleaning, but I draw the line at picking up your snotty-nosed kid from daycare. Even I have my limits.* I moved through my younger years assuming I had to be in charge in order to lead. And until I was in charge, I just needed to wait my turn.

One of my small joys in life is grocery shopping. Ever since our kids were old enough to sit up, they fawned over the grocery carts that look like little cars. Those carts are to grocery shopping what the iPad has become for the family road trip. How did we ever live without them? Game. Changer. Our kids still love sitting in the driver's seat of the cart-car. They love the feel of the steering wheel in their hands. They love the power of having control of the cart.

But then there is that inevitable moment. That moment when the kids in the cart-car, happily driving along, suddenly realize the steering wheel doesn't actually work. I'm cruising in the grocery store with my kids and they're turning the steering wheel as the cart turns. Everything is working just fine. Suddenly, the kids notice the greatest aisle in the store—the candy aisle. Like Fourth of July fireworks, the bright colors and attractive packaging are putting on a show. So as quick as their little appendages can move, they aggressively begin turning the wheel. *Left, left, left, left.* But much to their chagrin, the cart doesn't turn. It keeps moving straight ahead.

That's when they turn and look up at you with that "How could this happen?" expression. It's that dejected look of disappointment that screams, "You tricked me. This wheel doesn't work. It does nothing. It's useless. Completely useless. Kind of like you as a parent, Dad."

And we learn, at an early age, that *having the steering wheel is the only way to lead.* And if that steering wheel is not attached to authority and power, it just doesn't work. That's what we're taught by our life experiences. If we want the cart to move, we must be in control. We learn that the little wheel we're handed is just a toy and doesn't actually work. We think we must be in charge if we want to lead, if we want to turn the cart in a different direction. We come to see positional authority as a prerequisite for effective leadership.

EMBRACING THE MYTH

Tragically, I had to land the job I had always wanted before I realized I had bought into this myth. For almost twenty years now, I have attended and now work for a large network of churches. Just after turning thirty, I was given a pretty substantial promotion. I was asked to move to one of our larger locations and become the lead pastor of that campus. It was one of those moments when I thought, *Are you serious? I'm flattered, of course. However, I question your discernment because this job is huge and I secretly still want to be Puff Daddy's hype man.* Nonetheless, someone saw something in me that I didn't see in myself, and I'm forever grateful. The new role was literally a dream come true.

I stepped into that job as an eager young leader, ready to shape our church into what I hoped it could be. I had strong opinions about how we should operate to serve our community best. Unfortunately, over the years, I had drifted toward an unhealthy mindset, feeling like a victim whose ideas weren't valued or understood within the larger organization. I felt inhibited and constrained, like a tamed lion (or, at the very least, an eager meerkat) at the zoo, lying in my cage, having lost my ambition to lead.

I soon learned I was wrong, because as it turns out, the cage doesn't even exist.

At the time, I knew I wasn't leading to my full potential. But if you had asked me *why,* I would have played the victim and blamed the problems on the organization.

"They just have a way of doing things."

"They're not open to change."

"They just want me to fit in the mold, toe the line, and follow the rules."

I realize this might be true of some organizations. Many, perhaps. But it was not true of *our* organization. I was working (and still am) for a man named Andy Stanley. He's the son of a preacher, and he knows the frustration of feeling hamstrung by a large, fossilized organization. Andy has spent most of his life intentionally seeking to create a leadership culture where the people who are responsible for executing a decision are the ones with the authority to make the decision. I'll be the first to admit that our organization is not perfect, but we certainly aren't a place where those who want to lead and have gifts and ideas should feel frustrated and blocked. At North Point, if you aren't leading because you don't feel like you're in charge, it's no one's fault but your own. If our organization gravitates toward one end of the spectrum, it's toward freedom to lead and not high control.

I still remember the moment my excuses were exposed, and I realized I had been too focused on blaming others instead of actually leading. Thankfully, my exposure was less of a "Janet Jackson Super Bowl halftime show" moment and, instead, was more of a strong conviction of my need to change. It was a defining moment for me, drastically changing the way I thought about leadership. The story itself was not dramatic, but for some reason, it was exactly what I needed in order to see what I was not seeing.

I was meeting with Andy, who was now my boss, trying to explain why something we had done had not gone as expected—and why none of it was my fault. Our central organization had given our campus some content for a presentation, along with instructions for pulling it off, but it had not gone as planned. Again, they determined the direction and provided the curriculum. It was our job to execute. The question loomed large, like an elephant in the room: *"Why didn't this go well?"*

Confidently, passionately, and succinctly, I gave Andy three good reasons. The information had come to us late, the work given to us was sloppy, and the presentation was less than creative. I think I might have used the word "lame" to describe it. My argument was airtight: blame, blame, blame. It was clear that we were the victims. The failure of the presentation had nothing to do with us; it was someone else's fault. As I finished listing my reasons, I felt like Andy should probably be thanking us for doing our best with these less than great materials.

But that's not what he did. Instead, he patiently poked and prodded for a few more minutes, asking me some good, tough questions. He asked, "So if you didn't like the outline, why wouldn't you just change it to make it great?" As he asked and I answered, I began to smell the stink of my polluted thoughts. Like a surgeon removing a cancer, Andy's inquisition led me to a moment of insight. As we talked, I began to realize the problem was not with our organization at all. It was with me.

I could have sat there, confident I was a passive victim of the institutional machinery, blaming and making excuses all day long. Instead, I experienced a moment of deep self-awareness. The truth of a key leadership principle hit me like a ton of bricks. I bumped into it so abruptly that I sheepishly couldn't wait to leave his office.

Leaders don't sit back and point fingers. Leaders lead *with* the authority of leadership . . . or *without* it. The authority is largely irrelevant—if you are a leader, you will lead when you are needed.

My instinct to blame and deflect responsibility wasn't about having authority or a lack of authority. After all, I now had a position of some authority in our organization, a seat at the table. But over the years, I had fallen into the trap of thinking, *If only I had more authority, I could fix the problems I saw.* It wasn't more authority I needed. Instead, I needed to accept the authority I had and then use it wisely to cultivate influence and make things better. I had confused having authority with the responsibility of leading. I had not yet realized that we don't need authority to have influence. And I was reminded that I already had that. In fact, my hope is to convince you that you have it as well.

Perhaps you've experienced some of the same frustrations I've had as a leader. Or maybe you are not currently in a "position" of leadership in your organization, but you have ideas and vision for how things can be done better. If so, this book is written for you, for those who feel a calling to lead but are not in charge. We live in an authority-based culture where certain posi-

Influence has always been, and will always be, the currency of leadership.

tions possess an inherent authority and responsibility. But we all know that positional authority alone does not equate to effective leadership. If a leader does not inspire confidence, he or she will be unable to effect change without resorting to brute force. Influence has always been, and will always be, the currency of leadership. This book is about how to cultivate the influence needed to lead when you're not in charge.

SEEING IT EVERYWHERE

When I turned sixteen, I was hoping to get a brand-new whip (that's what rappers call a car) that would give me more cred with the ladies. Instead, my parents bought me an old, beat-up Volvo

240 DL. At first I was bummed, mostly because it reeked of Brut and mold. But after a few moments of pity, I remember thinking, *Well, it's one of a kind. If you can't be cool, at least be unique.* I'll never forget the first day I drove it to school. I pulled up to the stoplight, looked over my left shoulder, and saw the exact same car. Two minutes later, I passed another one. And as I pulled into the school parking lot, I counted six Volvo 240 DLs. *How could this be? I thought I would be unique! How could I have missed these cars in the past?*

Because I wasn't looking for them.

Once you become aware of something, you start seeing it everywhere. That moment with Andy was the flashlight I needed to expose the myth I had been carrying. As soon as the light bulb of leading through influence was turned on in my mind, I started seeing the truth of this principle *everywhere*. People lead all the time with little to no authority. Some of the most effective leaders—the people who have changed our world—led without formal authority.

Think about Martin Luther King, Jr. What was his title again? He was the copastor of Ebenezer Baptist Church and president of the Southern Christian Leadership Conference. While being the president of the SCLC implies some authority within the organization, that position alone doesn't give you the ability to effect change for all African Americans. But King wasn't bound by his position. He knew change would come about as the truth was brought to light and hearts and minds were exposed to a new paradigm, one that saw the worth and equal value of all people and did not judge them by the color of their skin. King led because that's what leaders do. They cultivate influence with a title or without a title.

Who put Nelson Mandela in charge of abolishing apartheid in South Africa? No one. But leaders do not need to be in charge to lead.

October 2 is now recognized as the International Day of Non-Violence. Why this day? Because that is the birthday of Mahatma Gandhi. Gandhi led a national revolt against one of the largest and most powerful governments in the world. But he had no formal position within the government. He has a title now, though, since India received its independence from Great Britain in 1947. Today, he's referred to as "the Father of the Nation."

These people didn't wait for a title to lead. And neither should you.

In his TED Talk "Why Good Leaders Make You Feel Safe," Simon Sinek explains, "Many people at the top of organizations are not leaders. They have authority, but they are not leaders. And many at the bottom with no authority are absolutely leaders."[1] Sinek is differentiating between authority and leadership and making the point that they are *not* a package deal. Leadership expert Jim Collins agrees. He writes, "For many people, the first question that occurs is, 'But how do I persuade my CEO to get it?' My answer: Don't worry about that . . . each of us can create a *pocket of greatness*. Each of us can take our own area of work and influence and can concentrate on moving it from good to great. It doesn't really matter whether all the CEOs get it. It only matters that you and I do. Now, it's time to get to work."[2]

Collins makes a great point here. Our focus doesn't have to be simply on persuading those in charge to effect change. You may be able to do that, and you may not. But what you can do is focus on your own area of responsibility and make it great. We need to avoid the trap of thinking we are passive victims with nothing we can do. Each of us can begin to lead right where we are today. Collins continues, "Take responsibility to make great what you can make great. And let others do it in the areas that they can make great. And if the whole company doesn't do it, you can't change that. But you can take responsibility for your area."

WIELDING THE GUN OF AUTHORITY

Maybe you've worked for people who have titles that give them authority over you, but they misunderstand why they have those titles. They've confused authority and leadership or misunderstood the way authority is intended to function in leadership. And they use their positions to make you feel small or to squeeze you for results, only to take the credit for your work. Or perhaps they shut down your ideas and won't respond to suggestions. I call this experience "being under the thumb." When others make us feel like we're under their thumbs because they're in charge and we're not, it sucks the ever-loving life out of us.

Most of us know what that feels like. When people have to tell you they're in charge in order for you to follow, you know instinctively that something has gone desperately wrong. When I was in college, I stumbled into an internship in the governor's office in Atlanta. My job was far from glorious, but my seat was in the front row, so I witnessed lots of activity as the governor geared up to enact new policies. My desk was directly outside the conference room in the policy department where they debated and made decisions. I'll never forget overhearing a particularly contentious meeting about the future of education in the State of Georgia. Voices in the conference room were growing louder and louder. Suddenly, a loud banging on the table silenced the room. A solitary voice screamed out over all the others, "I am the governor of the State of Georgia! Listen to me!"

At that point in my life, I regrettably had not read many leadership books. I had never been to a leadership conference. I would have had trouble defining words like *vision* and *mission*. But even I knew that something had gone wrong. When someone has to pull out the gun of authority, something is broken. You only pull out the gun of authority when nothing else is working.

The gun will get people moving, at least for a time. If someone pulled the gun of authority on you and threatened your job, would it get you moving? Of course it would! We all want food to eat and a place to live. And in the conference room that day, the gun seemed to work. But pulling the gun cannot be a regular practice. No one wants to follow someone who is holding a gun to their back. That's not leading. That's pushing people around and forcing them to go where they don't want to go. While there may be times when we need to do this, our goal is for people to *want* to follow us. Even Jack Bauer doesn't want to come to work with a gun to his head every day. Especially when there is another, more effective way to bring change.

While we cannot entirely disconnect authority from the leadership equation, I don't believe we should begin there. At one point during his ministry, Jesus warns his followers that they should not confuse a *position* of authority with a *call* to lead. Because they are in danger of getting this wrong, he abruptly makes a distinction between how he wants them to lead and the way things typically operate in the world. "Not so with you," he says (Matt. 20:26).

What is the "not so" of leadership that Jesus refers to here? It's the type of leader who seeks authority for personal gain. Instead, Jesus argues that the best leaders, the ones who align with his vision for leadership, will lead as servants who are aware of their responsibility and who answer to a higher calling.

Do you want to be a "not so with you" kind of leader? I hope so. I know what it looks and feels like to use the gun of authority to get people moving, but Jesus tells us there is another way—a better way. Even if you have authority and a position of leadership, an inspiring leader does not need to leverage that authority. "Not so with you" kind of leaders learn that there are more effective ways to cultivate influence and build trust. Jesus tells us this is a more powerful way to lead, one we can exercise regardless of the presence or absence of authority.

Earlier, I mentioned the examples of Martin Luther King, Jr., Nelson Mandela, and Mahatma Gandhi. These individuals effected lasting change with little formal authority. But this leadership principle isn't just true for cultural and political movements—it's also true within organizations. In a *Harvard Business Review* article titled "The Key to Change is Middle Management," Behnam Tabrizi writes that mid-level managers are the lynchpin of change within an organization. He finds that these managers do not necessarily have the authority to effect change, but *they can still make change happen.* "A hallmark of the successful 32% was the involvement of mid-level managers two or more levels below the CEO. In those cases, mid-level managers weren't merely managing incremental change; they were leading it by working levers of power up, across, and down in their organizations."[3]

How do these mid-level managers effect change? Tabrizi says they work the levers of power in every direction. They don't have authority over their peers, much less their bosses or the other executives in charge of the organization. So how do they do it? Through influence. The lie we believe is that we must wait until we're in the leader's seat before we can have this kind of influence. But the good news is that influence can (and should) be cultivated *wherever* you are. If you're able to grasp this truth as a leader today, it can prepare you for the future. But if you fail to cultivate influence when you're not in charge, you will have no influence to leverage when you are.

Influence always outpaces authority. And leaders who consistently leverage their *authority* to lead are far less effective in the long term than leaders who leverage their *influence*. Practice leading through influence when you're not in charge. It's the key to leading well when you are.

UNDERSTANDING WHAT'S AT STAKE

That day, as I sat in Andy's office responding to his questions, I decided I would try to be a different leader. I decided I was done using my lack of authority as an excuse to blame others. For too long, my attitude and my responses to problems reflected passivity, a sense that I was a victim of my circumstances. I had believed the lie that leading meant waiting until I had the authority to do whatever I wanted. But that day, I realized that just wasn't true.

Believing the lie that authority was a prerequisite for leadership deeply affected my attitude. It affected the way I thought about myself and the challenges I encountered. It affected my behavior as well. And it had a cost. For over a decade, while I was waiting for the authority to lead, I missed out on several opportunities I'll never get back. The fear of missing out (FOMO for those who love abbreviations) is not just a perceived fear—it can be reality. I really did miss out. I can't press rewind. I can't go back and try again. Those opportunities are now gone.

But even worse than that, waiting for the authority to lead slowly eroded the gifts of leadership that were inside me. Waiting didn't make me more of a leader; it made me less of a leader. And this is true for all of us, regardless of who you are. All human beings have a measure of leadership loaned to them. We may not immediately recognize it for what it is, but we each have the ability, as well as the opportunities, to influence others and effect change in this world. And the earlier we begin to fan the flame of the gift of influence, the more it will grow. Conversely, the longer we wait, mired in passivity and the sense that we are victims of circumstances and the decisions of others, the more likely we are to diminish and mute the leadership gifts within us. The more I sat back and watched things pass without taking initiative, the softer my voice became. Waiting for others to do something negatively affected the gift of leadership within me.

Each of us has a unique opportunity to create something *right where we are*. It doesn't require special authority or a fancy title or having the corner office. Even though I don't know you personally, I can guarantee you have an opportunity to create an oasis of excellence right where you are. Not only is it within you to lead, but it is possible for you to lead well! So don't shrink back until someone calls your number. But know that leading *without* authority is more difficult than leading with authority. It requires a level of self-awareness that few of us are ready to develop. Because leading without authority means you need to have a clear understanding of your identity—who you are as a leader, apart from any titles.

CHAPTER 2

IDENTITY
CRISIS

At the end of every year, organizations like the American Dialect Society, Merriam-Webster, and the Oxford University Press name a Word of the Year. This is the night when the stars of the word world hit the red carpet. It's the Oscars of words.

In 2015, dictionary.com named *identity* as their Word of the Year. I bet the words that gave birth to *identity* were elated. Evidently, the people of dictionary.com had made their decision after spending some time looking through the headlines. Because that year saw article after article wrestling with some of the most complicated and discussed questions of our day— questions about identity.

- Is it possible for a person to have been born to white parents but *identify* as black? Rachel Dolezal seemed to think so.
- When people *identify* with a gender other than the one they were identified as at birth, which bathroom should they be allowed to use? Houston, Texas, took a citywide vote on this question.
- If a government clerk identifies as a Christian, should her *identity* as a Christian allow her to refuse issuing licenses

for same-sex marriage? In Rowan County, Kentucky, Kim Davis went to jail because she believed so.

Questions about identity are front and center in our society. Should we be surprised? Few things are as crucial to who you are than how you see yourself and how others see you. The problem with identity is that it's . . . squishy. Like Jell-O, it's challenging to pin to the wall. Psychologists Erik Erikson, Carl Jung, and Sigmund Freud dedicated their careers to countless hours of research and wrote volumes of theories to answer what identity is and is not. So maybe you're thinking, *With all of this top-level research, do you think you have something to add to the conversation?* I believe I do. Actually, I believe we all do.

Near the core of what makes a person a leader is their sense of identity. The way you see yourself is determinative for your life and for the decisions you make as a leader. Your sense of identity directs you in every situation. It is foundational, determining the level of confidence you have when you challenge your boss in a disagreement. It establishes your sense of security when you face doubts. It's what enables you to process your emotions during tense conversations. Though much of your identity is formed at an early age, your identity is always evolving. So it's never too early or too late to begin processing your sense of self.

> Near the core of what makes a person a leader is their sense of identity.

Your personal identity is even more crucial when you're determining how best to lead *when you're not in charge.* Most people in this situation focus on learning new behaviors to compensate for a lack of authority, but the challenge goes deeper than that. Leading well without formal authority has less to do with your *behavior* and far more to do with your *identity*. Like the ace of spades, *who we are* trumps *what we do* every time.

During that crucible of clarity a few years ago in Andy's office, I processed a full swath of emotions. On one side, I felt insecure and inadequate, looking for the nearest corner to ball up into. *Do I have what it takes to lead well? I think I've been passively avoiding doing what I need to do to lead well. Is it because I don't have what it takes to lead well? I've been put in this position. I don't deserve it. I haven't actually done anything to warrant this opportunity. What if I'm exposed as a counterfeit leader? What if I can't do this?*

On the other side, I could feel my pride being threatened, and I wanted to rise up and defend myself. *How dare you question my ability to lead! Do you know how difficult it is to exist in your shadow? Do you know the frustrations that come with trying to navigate the complexity of this organization? If only I were in charge . . . I'm not exactly sure what I would do, but I wouldn't make people feel this way.*

I have found that amid swirling emotions, my ability to calmly process my thoughts with awareness and emotional intelligence is largely dependent on the security of my identity. It's as if all the work I have or haven't done to see myself accurately comes to call in that moment. If I've spent too much time dwelling on my failures and inadequacies, it will show in my response. If I've spent too much time re-watching my own highlights, it will also show. If identity is anything, it's everything.

I'll tell you this right now: every distortion between the authority you have and the leadership you exercise can be traced to a crisis of identity. Whether it's the "under the thumb" authoritarian or the power-hungry ladder-climber or the passively reluctant leader, every leadership distortion is ultimately rooted in the ever-so-important chamber of identity. How we see ourselves affects our ability to follow others, our ability to lead others, and our ability to find the future God has for us. And until you know who you are, you cannot do what God has called you to do. As we will see in this chapter, before God pushes men and women into the call of duty, he shapes and molds their character by speaking into their identities. He has done that with me, and I believe he wants to do the same with you.

Kurt Vonnegut famously said, "I am a human being, not a human doing." Vonnegut was an avowed atheist and president of the American Humanist Association, but his observation parallels the orthodox Christian view of how God created us. We were crafted in God's image to *be* something before we were given any mandates to do something. This tells us something about God, but it also says much about how God sees us. Another way to say this is that our identities precede our actions; our behaviors flow from our identities. So before we spend any energy on what we do as leaders, we really need to spend some time on who we are as leaders, especially when we are not the ones in charge.

THE CONSEQUENCES OF MISTAKEN IDENTITY

Are there certain movies you just can't resist watching when you run across them while channel surfing? For me, it's any of the *Bourne* movies, *A Few Good Men*, and *Catch Me If You Can*. These movies are like communal pizza. It's hard to just have one slice when there are more available. These are actual "Netflix and Chill" movies, in the purest sense of the term. *Catch Me If You Can* might have a leg up on the others because it's based on a true story. Frank, if you're reading this, let's hang sometime. Here's a quick synopsis of the story line in case your church has recently been boycotting Hollywood:

> Frank Abagnale, Jr. (Leonardo DiCaprio) grew up in a home where impressing his father was everything to him. His appetite for approval and his thirst for thrills drove him to impersonate a doctor, a lawyer, and a copilot for a major airline. And he did all of this before his eighteenth birthday. As a master of deception, Frank not only bounced from career to career, but he also brilliantly forged checks to the tune of millions of dollars. All of this led to a cat-and-mouse game between Frank and FBI agent Carl Hanratty (Tom Hanks). Carl made it his mission to capture Frank, but Frank was always one step ahead.

This movie is all about identity. As Frank struggled to find himself, he chased everything he wanted to be. Like so many of us, Frank was chasing a particular identity because of his desire to please someone else. In his case, he was trying to make his father proud. Seems innocent enough, right? Unfortunately, trying to make their fathers proud is just one of the traps young leaders fall into when they don't have a firmly established identity. But that's not the only one.

I've found there are three common identity traps that snag young leaders, especially when they are trying to lead without being in charge. We've all been guilty of choosing from multiple passports, using a fake ID, or misrepresenting height and weight on a driver's license. Here's what I mean by each of these.

CHOOSING FROM MULTIPLE PASSPORTS

Early in the movie *The Bourne Identity*, Jason Bourne walks into a Zurich bank. The only clue he has to his identity is this:

> 000–7–17–12–0–14–26
> Gemeinschaft Bank
> Zurich

Because he suffers from dissociative amnesia, Bourne knows nothing of his real identity other than the fact that he was fluent in several languages and had some sick combat skills. Wearing a loose-fitting zip-up sweater, Bourne craftily works his way through the bank, finds privacy to open the safe-deposit box, and realizes his picture, with different names, is attached to multiple passports from multiple countries. I love that scene because it's so easy to get wrapped up in the identity crisis Bourne is having.

Unless you work for the CIA (or have dual citizenship), you've probably never had to flip through multiple passports to decide who you are going to be for the day. Unfortunately though, many young leaders can relate to changing their identity to fit their circumstances. Attempting to be outgoing because you think it will make your boss happy isn't healthy. We've all seen the person who tries to be the funny guy because he thinks that will allow him to fit in. We've all seen the girl who tries to be the boss when the boss walks out of the room because she thinks that's what leadership is. Choosing an identity based on the situation and circumstances might have worked for Jason Bourne, but it won't work for you.

It's one thing to determine what posture and approach fits the circumstances you're facing. It's another thing for the instability of your identity to create wobble in your persona because you're trying to fit in or because you think it'll help you win. We've all felt the pressure to be who others want us to be. Most of us faced this temptation in middle school. Sadly, it doesn't end there. It doesn't matter if you are the President of the United States or a mentor to high school students—if your identity is unstable, you'll subconsciously flip through identities to find the one you think others need you to be.

USING A FAKE ID

Though some may not believe this based on my grade point average, I wasn't a big drinker while attending Georgia Tech. But one night I used a fake ID to get into the local bar called Moondogs. This bar was so popular among students that the church across the street was nicknamed Moondogs Methodist (that still makes me laugh). Pulling my hat down low on a Thursday night, I anxiously stood in line before the supersized bouncer, trying to memorize the address, height, and weight of the dude I was pretending to be. I got in, but I had to sweat through an uncomfortable fifteen seconds while the bouncer looked me over and examined my ID.

Pretenders don't last very long. Standing in line with my fake ID wasn't just a compromise of my integrity; it created real anxiety for me. I wasn't comfortable pretending, and I knew deep down that pretending wouldn't work well for me in the long term. Yet the truth is that you and I pretend all the time, especially when we're under pressure. We do this by projecting an image that we have it all together. We work longer hours to make sure we're seen as proficient and committed. Most of the time, these things are so subtle that we don't even notice we're doing them. But we find clues in the nuances of how we tell a story, what details we share and don't share with others, and who we blame when something goes wrong.

No one wants to be known as a pretender. For teenagers, college students, and young leaders, being called "fake" is an egregious insult. Because of that, I've seen many young leaders admit weaknesses in the name of keeping it real. I love the authenticity of that. But we have to find the balance between authentically admitting our weaknesses and excusing weaknesses. Too many young leaders use phrases like "That's just who I am" or "They just need to know that's how I've always been" to excuse areas of potential growth.

Why are we so tempted to pretend? Using a fake ID is a form of hiding who we are that began back in the Garden of Eden. After Adam disobeys God's command and eats from the Tree of Knowledge of Good and Evil in Genesis 3, God looks for Adam and asks him where he's been. Adam responds by saying, "I heard you in the garden, and I was afraid because I was naked; *so I hid*" (Gen. 3:10, emphasis mine). Because he had broken trust with God, Adam was hiding and didn't want to be found or known by God. Pretending (or hiding ourselves from God and others) is a spiritual issue. It's rooted in a failure of trust, a failure to believe what God says about us. I'll get to that in a bit. For now, we can all agree that pretending is a consequence of the fall.

MISREPRESENTING HEIGHT AND WEIGHT ON A DRIVER'S LICENSE

Don't we all exaggerate our height and weight on our driver's license . . . just a little bit? I had always assumed so. For the longest time, I continued to live in a time warp, thinking I was still a college student. My driver's license indicated that I weighed 165 pounds, and when the time came to renew, I just added another ten pounds and called it good. I was pretty sure I had gained an inch or two around the waist, but who needs to actually measure these things?

The consequences of being "generous" on your driver's license are minimal. But being overly generous with the way you see yourself—your self-identity—can have far more significant consequences. And it can go two ways. Honestly, I don't know which is more damaging—being too critical or thinking too highly of yourself. Either way, accepting a distorted identity is failing to live in reality, which will ultimately erode your ability to lead.

Paul speaks directly to this problem in Romans 12:3 (emphasis mine), "For by the grace given me I say to every one of you: *Do not think of yourself more highly than you ought*, but rather think of yourself with sober judgment, in accordance with the faith God has distributed to each of you." A distorted identity will cause you to think too lowly or too highly of yourself, when the goal is to think *rightly*. If you think too lowly, you will often see yourself as unqualified or unworthy of leadership, and you will miss opportunities to make change and create something great with the responsibility you've been given. If you think too highly of yourself, you will tend to overestimate your abilities and may even take credit for the work of others in an effort to promote yourself. You'll tend to hide your mistakes and make much of your successes, and you'll live in constant fear of being exposed as a fraud.

Finding the correct identity is a constant challenge for every human on the planet. The temptation of choosing from multiple passports, using a fake ID, or misrepresenting height and weight will never go away, but when your identity is rooted in something, you are much more likely to live and lead from a place of stability and security. The rest of this chapter is an attempt to pour concrete on the identity that will lead to the best version of you.

THIS IS US: THE ARCHITECTURE OF IDENTITY

As you can see, your self-identity is complicated, so let's put it in simple terms: *your identity is the conception you have of yourself.* It is those core beliefs about yourself that you tell yourself all day long. The most important ongoing conversation you have in your life is the one you have with yourself every day.

There are five basic components of identity, and to help you remember them, I've made sure they all start with the letter "P." They are your past, your people, your personality, your purpose, and your priorities. Let's take a closer look at each one.

Your Past

Your family plays a large role in sculpting your identity. And this includes factors like your race, your socioeconomic class, your citizenship, and your gender. How you see your family of origin and the lineage of people from which you've come determines the constancy and consistency of your identity.

This is your *self-in-time.*

When I think about my family of origin, I notice a few key factors that have strongly influenced how I see myself. I have great parents. My father is a man of exceptional character. As a kid, I always respected his ability to identify the right thing to do and the best attitude to display. My mother is the captain of my cheerleading squad. Someone once told me that Alexander the Great's mother, Olympias, repeatedly told him he was the son of a god. We all know he wasn't (he was the son of Philip II of Macedonia), but his mom obnoxiously believed far more about him than he even believed about himself. My mom never told me I was the son of a god, but her faith in my abilities and my potential was a powerful force in shaping my identity. Her wind in my sails pushed me ahead on days when I would've packed it up and gone home.

For those of us who are Christians, we cannot neglect to mention that great and sometimes not-so-great cloud of witnesses (listed for us by the unknown author of Hebrews) that has preceded us. My faith in God and the examples of those who have come before me have had a profound influence on my life. The more I've processed my own identity, the more I've been able to identify some of these important voices from my past.

How has your past shaped how you see yourself? A worthwhile exercise to help you find your self-in-time would be to chart your life on a timeline by picking five highs and five lows from your past and marking them chronologically. If you've never done this, it's a great exercise to do with a team or a group.

Your People

Your identity is not just a matter of how you perceive yourself based on your past, but it's also based on how you sense others perceive you *today*. The people you're surrounded by in your existing relationships and roles distinctly shape who you are in the here and now. Have you ever felt like you were a different person in different seasons of your life? We've all had that experience and it's because who we're around in different seasons of life has such a profound impact on who we are. The people we are in relationship with greatly affect how we see ourselves.

This is your *self-in-relationships*.

I was recently speaking with a good friend who was telling me that he felt like he was "losing himself in his new job." As we processed this together, he began to identify how the people he was working with in this particular organization were toxic for him. Their values were so opposed to his, and that constant pressure and tension were deeply affecting him. We'd all like to think that the people around us don't change how we see ourselves—that we are in complete control of our identity—but that's just not true.

Who are the people around you right now, and how are they affecting you and the way you see yourself? Who is in your corner? Who shouldn't be in your corner? Who are the loudest voices speaking into your life right now? Who *should* be the loudest voices for you right now? Pay attention to those voices and to their volume. Many of them are shaping your identity and, in some cases, you may not even be aware of how it's affecting you.

Your Personality

We are all born with some hardwired realities that also shape our identity. Our physical bodies, our characteristics and traits, our emotional and impulsive lives, and our talents and skills all shape how we experience life. This in turn shapes our self-perception. If you're highly ambitious and driven by achievement, yet find yourself in a role or organization that is static and doesn't offer opportunities for growth or development, you're going to be frustrated. If you excel administratively and have a deep desire to sit at your desk, focus on your work, and knock stuff out, but the organization you're working with is highly relational, you're going to feel like you're constantly letting others down. What's most challenging is when you lack self-understanding and it isn't clear to you how your wiring affects how you see yourself.

This is your *self-interior.*

How are your temperament and personality wired? There are several ways for you to discover this. You can use RightPath, Myers-Briggs, StrengthsFinder, or Taylor-Johnson. In our organization, we think it is crucial to understand your personality, your bent, and your giftedness. Because of this, we dedicate loads of resources to assist people on this journey of self-discovery. With every person we interview, we use RightPath and StrengthsFinder. Just about every team in our organization has employed an expert on one of these assessments to facilitate a conversation around each person's profile and how to work with others with different profiles. Why do we spend so much time and effort on self-awareness? Because the more you understand the makeup of your personality, the better you can understand how your identity shapes your thoughts, desires, and decisions, and the better you'll be able to work with others.

Your Purpose

We were all created to have a purpose, but let's go one step further. We were all created to *thirst* for a purpose. Every one of us has a desire to see and understand how our lives fit into a bigger picture. Every one of us has been hardwired to desire a reason for our existence. *Why am I here? What can I uniquely contribute to the world?* These kinds of existential questions have more of an impact on our identity than we admit. What you believe about why you're on earth will deeply affect the opportunities you see available to you and how you should capitalize on them with your time, gifts, talents, and energy.

This is your *self-agency*.

What is your unique purpose in this world? The answer doesn't usually just drop into your lap one day. Rather, you discern it over a lifetime. But it's not something you will sit back and passively discover. You need to spend time wrestling this one to the ground. Full disclosure: over the years, this has created some real insecurity in me because I've never sensed a personal and specific mission for my life. In the church world, we designate this a "calling." But that term "calling" really frustrates me because I've seen how well-meaning people hijack it and use it for selfish manipulation. I only know a few men and women who have a specific and personal purpose or mission statement. For the rest of us, I believe God has revealed enough of his general purposes in this world for us to chew on for the rest of our lives.

So what has God said about why you exist? Have you spent time determining what success looks like in your life? I can tell you this:

- You were created for something or someone bigger than yourself.
- You were created to contribute to a greater good.
- You were created to bring good to other people.
- You were created to cultivate good in other people.
- You certainly have a mission greater than making yourself happy.

The degree to which you understand and feel a purpose for your life will affect the degree of security you have in your identity.

Your Priorities

The last item that determines your identity is your sense of priorities. I'm not necessarily referring to how you prioritize your life in regard to family, work, friends, etc. I'm referring to your priority of truths that shape your identity. This is where your faith—or lack thereof—comes most clearly into play. God has something to say about our priorities—our most important ideals, beliefs, aspirations, values, and passions. And your priorities will shape how you see yourself. While much of our identity is a result of the context and circumstances we are born into, this is an aspect of your identity formation that you *can* exert some control over.

This is your *self-determination*.

In other words, it's when we exercise our will to make decisions and determine what we allow to define us. We decide what's most important about who we are. In my life, there have been two key values I hold on to dearly, and these beliefs have held on to me in the midst of failures and successes. The two truths that have had more impact on my identity than anything else are:

1. Because I have been created in the image of God, I am a chosen child of the King.
2. *For God so loved* me that Jesus died for me.

You'll need to determine your own priorities. What do you choose to believe is most important about you? What ideal or value do you want to prioritize about yourself? This aspect of your identity is less determined than the others, and it takes effort to set these priorities and hold to them. You must learn to discipline yourself to keep these beliefs in front of you so they can continually shape your identity.

You are you and no one else but you. However, that doesn't mean you should passively accept your identity as something fixed and unchangeable. It's worth your time to wade through the various aspects of your identity to better understand them, to grow in self-awareness, and to determine what is true about you.

The *clearer* you are about who you are . . .

- the more *consistent* you will be with others.
- the more *confident* you will be about what you do.
- the less *concerned* you will be with the opinions of others.
- the less *confused* you will be by your emotions.

THE VOICES SHAPING YOUR IDENTITY

The longer I'm involved in church ministry, the more aware I am of how much time we spend talking about how music sounds, especially in what some call rock-n-roll church. It's been one of the great surprises in my work life. (Time spent talking about how the music sounds is surpassed only by time spent talking about T-shirt designs. If you've spent any time in student ministry, you know what I mean.) For sound, I've found that opinions around an audio mix from Sunday's service can eat up an entire Monday morning meeting.

"Did you think that mix had too much bass?"

"Why could I not hear the guitars more?"

"It just sounded a little muddy yesterday."

The more I've learned about music and the more concerts I've attended, the more I've come to see how important the audio mix is for the experience of the attendee. But there is another audio mix, one most of us never hear, that is even more important than the one we do hear. It's the mix that happens inside the earpiece or monitor for each musician. Typically, each musician has a pair of in-ear speakers with a unique mix that has been created just for that musician. During rehearsal, I'll hear them dialing it in.

"I need more guitar, less vocals."

"The keys are too hot in my ears."

"Can I hear more of her and less of the snare?"

In any environment, whether in the church world or at a concert, where the music is working well, a true musician will tell you, "Yeah, the monitor engineer did such a great job with the mix in our ears today." The musicians know that a great monitor engineer is the secret to a great musical experience for the crowd. The monitor engineer gives each musician what he or she needs to be able to perform and participate with one another.

When it comes to our identity, each of us gets to play the role of monitor engineer. We are responsible for the particular mix we're hearing. There are some things we can't change and others that we can. There are many voices speaking into the mix of our identity and we need to keep our fingers on the dials and faders to create the best mix. More boss, less past. More Dad, less spouse. More mentor, less social media. Some people are tempted to reach for the mute button, but that's not always the best option. While there are voices you should mute, most of the time all that's required is a simple adjustment of the volume to find the right mix. Don't mute the voice of your boss, spouse, mentor, or pastor, but the volume of his or her voice might need to be turned down.

I don't claim to know the mix that's right for you. I don't know what you need to turn up and what you need to turn down. But with the help of your community or possibly a professional counselor or coach, you can figure it out. *You need to figure it out.* One thing I can tell you is that no matter how loud God's voice is right now, you probably need to turn it up higher. The reality of this world is such that most of the voices we hear, even some of the good ones, can cloud out the voice we most desperately need to hear—the voice of God. And your identity will be best shaped if you allow your heavenly Father's voice to be the loudest one in your life. Your identity is the right identity when you let it be defined by what God says about you.

WHAT GOD SAYS ABOUT YOUR IDENTITY

God has a lot to say about your identity. And nothing has affected my leadership more than listening to what God has to say about my identity. When we survey the history of God's people, there are many moments when he speaks into a person's identity for the purpose of equipping them for more influence. Remember the burning bush? How could you forget it? God uses a lighter fluid-soaked bush to grab Moses's attention. "There the angel of the LORD appeared to him in flames of fire from within a bush. Moses saw that though the bush was on fire it did not burn up" (Ex. 3:2).

This has all the trappings of a stellar moment: the appearance of an angel, and not just any angel, but an "angel of the LORD." And there is a magic bush and (cue Tom Hanks from

Castaway) *fire*!!! And what does God want to say to Moses through this conversation? Here's my paraphrase:

"I know your weaknesses. I know what you're not good at. I know you stutter. I know you're scared. I know you're insecure. I know your past. I know about it all. But I don't want that to define you. You have what it takes! Well, you don't have what it takes, but because I'm going to be with you, you have what it takes! Now go! And quit worrying about who you are not and focus on who I AM!"

There's an identity check we all need to pay attention to. But this wasn't the first time Moses's identity had been shaped by what God said about him. I love what the author of Hebrews says about Moses's identity early in his life. "By faith Moses, when he had grown up, refused to be known as the son of Pharaoh's daughter. He chose to be mistreated along with the people of God rather than to enjoy the fleeting pleasures of sin" (Heb. 11:24–25). Moses refused to let others define him. He said no to what would've been an easy identification so he could say yes to the identity God wanted for him.

Or consider the story of Gideon. When Gideon jumps into the scene in the book of Judges, we find him scared to death, hiding from his enemies in a winepress. "The angel of the LORD came and sat down under the oak in Ophrah that belonged to Joash the Abiezrite, where his son Gideon was threshing wheat in a winepress to keep it from the Midianites" (Judg. 6:11).

Gideon was like the middle school kid hiding in the bathroom stall, hoping the bully wouldn't steal his lunch. He's threshing his wheat in the oddest of places—a winepress—so the Midianites wouldn't see him and take it all away from him. Now, I don't know how you thresh your wheat or what you know about wheat threshing in general, but it was quite odd to thresh wheat in a winepress because of how wheat is typically threshed. Wind is an essential component to wheat threshing. It helps separate the wheat from the chaff. Because of that, wheat would have been threshed on the top of a hill, not down in the pit of a winepress.

Why does this matter? Because it reveals what Gideon was thinking and how he was seeing. How did Gideon see himself? He seems insecure, lacking confidence, and possibly feeling helpless and just plain scared. But even though he is hiding out like a wimp in a winepress, God has something to say about his identity. "When the angel of the LORD appeared to Gideon, he said, 'The LORD is with you, mighty warrior'" (Judg. 6:12).

Mighty warrior? Was the angel confused? Did the angel mess up the game of telephone? Or was God calling Gideon to believe something about himself that he didn't currently believe? God was speaking truth into Gideon's identity, asking him to believe something that would change the way he led.

Only a few short months later, we find Gideon talking with MMA-level smack, roaming around the countryside, making threats like he's Brock Lesnar. Just two short chapters later, when the officials of Sukkoth (which is officially the worst name of any city . . . why doth our land values sukkoth such in Sukkoth?) refused to give bread to his troops, here's what Gideon says to them: "Just for that, when the LORD has given Zebah and Zalmunna into my hand, I will tear your flesh with desert thorns and briers" (Judg. 8:7).

"I will tear your flesh with thorns and briers." Where did that come from? I trace his newfound confidence back to what

God said to him through the angel of the Lord. Gideon is now, indeed, a mighty warrior.

Let me say it again: your identity is healthiest when what God says about you is most true of you.

FEARLESS LEADERSHIP

I want to be a fearless leader. Whether I'm in charge or not, I want to be ruthlessly committed to doing what is best to help others, whether it helps me move toward a promotion or not. When there is wobble in my identity, I step out of the house in the morning lacking the confidence to be the leader I want to be. Worse, I step out of the house lacking the confidence to be the leader *God has called me to be*. Here is a key truth about your identity as it relates to your leadership: *If you fail to believe what God says about your identity, you will fail to reach the potential he's put in you as a leader.* Your ability to be a fearless leader is squarely rooted in your identity.

I have a professional coach named Dean. He has a unique ability to wade through the superficial and get to the core of what is really going on inside me when I'm failing to lead like I want to lead. Several of us at North Point meet with Dean, so we have a common phrase for these meetings around our office: "You've been Dean-ed."

At one of these meetings, I was explaining a situation with a boss, and Dean pointed me toward a scene in the movie *First Knight*.[1] It's the story of King Arthur, Lancelot, and a Knight of the Round Table. In the movie, Richard Gere plays Lancelot, and he is jousting with a guy named Mark, a redheaded beast of a man who is quite a bit larger than Lancelot. You can sense

Lancelot questioning whether he has what it takes, when he suddenly makes a few moves and ends up with Mark's sword. It's quite impressive. Mark wants to know how Lancelot did what he did.

> **Mark:** Was that a trick?
>
> **Lancelot:** No. That's the way I fight.
>
> **Mark:** Could I do it? Tell me. I can learn.
>
> **Lancelot:** You have to study your opponent, so you know what he'll do before he does it.
>
> **Mark:** I can do that.
>
> **Lancelot:** You have to know that one moment in every fight when you win or lose. And you have to wait for it.
>
> **Mark:** I can do that.
>
> **Lancelot:** And you have to not care whether you live or die.

That last line is the one that matters most. "You have to not care whether you live or die." The takeaway for us, as leaders, is to recognize that the best leaders may or may not have all the authority they need or want, but the security of their identity—especially as someone called and loved by God—gives them a freedom and fearlessness to do what is right. They are able to challenge well, to lead by making a way even when there isn't a way.

Jesus followers should understand this, but more often than not, we are as guilty as anyone of letting our fear paralyze us. If you believe God actually controls your career, what place does fear have in your life? This doesn't mean we should be reckless. If anything, it means we have the freedom to be more disciplined and patient. We aren't subject to the frustrations and passions we might experience on a given day; we take the long view and trust that God has a plan. When God is informing your identity, he may call you to honor your boss even more, but you'll also have the freedom to challenge him with good intentions, unafraid to speak truth when necessary.

There are moments when I know I *want* to challenge my boss. There are moments when I know I *need* to challenge my boss. In some of those moments, I hesitate because, in wisdom, it may not be the right time or the matter is too small to bring up. There are also moments when wisdom dictates that I should say something, and I shrink back in fear. Every time we respond in fear, we miss an opportunity to lead, and this failure of leadership is an issue of identity. When fear keeps me from "leading up" like I know I need to, it is due to a distortion in my identity. Fear has overcome who I know I could be or should be.

But what do we do about it? If you sense fear in yourself, the best way to face those fears is with *a healthier sense of self.* You turn up the volume of what is true about you, and you listen to what God says about you. As you do, your identity will adjust. And as you adjust your identity, you will also adjust your response to fear. "There is no fear in love. But perfect love drives out fear, because fear has to do with punishment. The one who fears is not made perfect in love" (1 John 4:18). This verse captures one of the most radical truths we can know as a child of God. When I realize how perfectly loved I am, what is there to be afraid of? If I'm perfectly loved, why not embrace risk? If I'm perfectly loved, why do I need the stamp of approval from others? If I'm perfectly loved, why would I fear failure or the uncertainty of potential outcomes?

Fear thrives in the absence of love. Fear will dominate your identity until you begin to stand under the unending, never-failing, ever-gracious waterfall of love that your Creator has for you. He holds your future. He loves you perfectly. He accepts you unconditionally. Lead like you believe this to be true.

CAPTIVE THOUGHTS

For many years before my current role working with Andy and leading our largest church campus, I worked with teenagers. One of the great frustrations of working with teenagers is that they are constantly ruled by their feelings. There was a high school student in our church who looked like Tim Tebow meets Jimmy "Superfly" Snuka from 1980s WWF. He was a big kid, very smart, with a fun personality. I was listening to him share how depressed he'd been feeling. And he knew the source of his depression. He shared with me how awful social media was making him feel. I could sense the pain that his thoughts and feelings were causing him and I wanted to help. So I gave him the best advice I knew to give.

"Stop it.

"Just stop looking at social media. Delete the apps. Stop having those thoughts. Stop feeling those feelings. Just stop. It's that simple. Stop."

(I've been told I have the gift of mercy, but I've actually never taken the spiritual gifts test so I'm holding out until I do before I make any judgments.)

Like this student, many of us tend to be passive with our thoughts and feelings. We treat them like they rule us, like they are in charge of us, and not the other way around. We forget that our thoughts and feelings are *our* thoughts and feelings. We own them. They do not own us. At least they shouldn't, and that's where we may need to exercise a little ownership over them. You don't have to allow thoughts of fear, inadequacy, and insecurity to take up residence in your mind. If you do, they will slowly erode your identity and render you ineffective as a leader. But it's not just me telling you to do something about this. If you are a follower of Jesus, you have been instructed to exert your ownership and take those thoughts captive. "We demolish arguments and every pretension that sets itself up against the knowledge of God, and we take captive every thought to make it obedient to Christ" (2 Cor. 10:5).

Too many people deal with their thoughts and feelings like a maître d' at a restaurant. *Welcome, sir. Mr. Inadequacy, how many in your party? Is it just you or are you expecting more? We're pretty full tonight, but we will do our best to find you a table since you've gone to the trouble of showing up.* We don't have to do that. If we believe these thoughts damage our identity, we will be more aggressive in responding. Instead of a maître d', we need to treat our thoughts and feelings of fear, inadequacy, and insecurity like we're Liam Neeson in *Taken*.

> I don't know who you are. I don't know what you want. If you are looking for ransom, I can tell you I don't have money. But what I do have is a very particular set of skills, skills I have acquired over a very long career. Skills that make me a nightmare for people like you. If you let my daughter go now, that'll be the end of it. I will not look for you. I will not pursue you. But if you don't, I will look for you. I will find you. And I will kill you.[2]

Our thoughts and feelings are liars. They're trying to tell us something that is not true. Elevating the voice of God above the volume of these lies is essential to allowing God to form a healthy sense of identity in you.

DARKROOM DEVELOPMENT

Here's the good news. If you don't have a clear picture of your future and you are feeling stuck or frustrated, I want to encourage you to not lose sight of the ways you're developing *right now*. What you're doing *now* as a leader, even if you're not in charge, is incredibly important. You're developing.

The old-school photographers *develop* their pictures, and that development happens in darkrooms. If you feel you're in a darkroom of your life, don't lose sight of the development that is happening. Just because you can't see the tangible results from what's happening right now, you need to trust that your identity is taking shape. And there are things you can choose to do—how you respond to your boss, to your coworkers, to your circumstances, to your thoughts and emotions, and to God—that will shape and determine your future as a leader.

One of the areas you may still need to address, however, is the question of ambition. Do you have a desire to lead? A hunger to see things change? Some young leaders fear that hunger and avoid it until they are in the position to do something about it. Other leaders give in to the hunger, but they do it in an unhealthy way that is selfish and self-centered. In the next chapter, we'll take a look at how to approach our ambition in a healthy way.

CHAPTER 3

RECLAIM
KIBOSH

By my estimation, you'll spend half of your waking hours at work. That makes your working world pretty significant. Thanks, Captain Obvious. Hopefully, that's one of the reasons this type of book was attractive to you. Though the title of this book begins with "How to," I'm keenly aware there is so much more to what you're doing on a day-to-day basis as a leader than a bunch of "how to's." So, before we dive into the *how* of leading when you're not in charge, we need to spend some time on the *why*.

The *why* of leadership is the engine that drives your leadership train. You are motivated by something inside of you, and you need to know what that is. When that engine goes awry, you should stop, give up your seat, get off at the nearest station, and find a super contemplative coffee shop to do some serious thinking. A distortion in motivation will limit your leadership and cause a host of issues that will follow you wherever your professional life takes you.

The distortion I see for many young leaders revolves around one word: *ambition.* I call it a distortion for a reason. I believe God has placed desires inside of us: a desire for more, a desire to see things change, a desire to make things better, and a desire to lead. But those desires can easily get twisted. And when the ambition inside us is distorted, it affects every aspect of our leadership.

AMBITION DEFINED

Handling the hunger of ambition is tricky for any young leader. Knowing how to handle ambition as Jesus followers is even trickier. The presence of ambition in a young Christian leader is complicated by oft-distorted understandings of what it means to pursue ambition as a Christ follower. Faith leaders are all over the map on this subject, and it produces all kinds of flawed leadership paradigms. I've heard some leaders say it's wrong to follow your ambitions, while others have said we need to be more ambitious. I've seen ambition destroy leaders, and I've seen it motivate leaders to do the seemingly impossible. This diversity of views on this topic complicates what we think when we feel the drive of ambition in our hearts.

Here's what I know to be true: we all have ambition inside us. Don't try to deny it. What you do with that ambition will make all the difference in your ability to lead when you're not in charge. How you currently think about the ambition inside you is the product of your personal wiring and your past mentors. But what you do with that ambition going forward is on you.

When I talk to young leaders on the topic of ambition, I get lots of questions.

"Is it even okay to have ambition?"

"Is God okay with ambition?"

"Would he prefer I have less ambition?"

"Or does he want me to be more ambitious?"

So let's start with a simple definition. What is ambition? I define ambition as that strong desire we have to make something or to achieve something, even when it takes great effort, focus, and determination. It's worth paying attention to that hunger you have because it's not necessarily a bad thing. In fact, it's a key part of the drive that moves you to cultivate influence. The desire of ambition can take many forms. It can be the desire in you to:

Create beautiful art.

Help others reach their potential.

Build space for kids to get off the streets.

Establish a platform to give a voice to the voiceless.

Produce a large event for those who have written off Jesus.

In its purest form, there's nothing wrong with ambition. It's one of the hallmarks of leadership. Do you feel it? Drink it in, because it's good. Ambition is what drives us to want more opportunities, to have more influence, and to contribute to the overall mission of life with greater impact. The problem for many leaders is that they do not know what to do with that drive. Letting it run wild can be disastrous, but putting it on mute doesn't work either. I've tried both. I'll bet you have too.

Even though leaders need this drive to lead, ambition doesn't wait for authority to show up. *Ambition doesn't magically begin when you are placed in charge.* Believing that you need a position of authority to exercise your ambition is a lie, and as soon as that lie takes root in you, you will find yourself losing the influence you desire to cultivate and develop. Worse, failing to direct your

> Ambition doesn't magically begin when you are placed in charge.

ambition in good and healthy ways can twist it, and something meant for good can be co-opted by a selfish motive or a narrow focus that is of no benefit to anyone but you.

The distortions of our ambition can be simplified into two extremes. Like a swinging pendulum, these two manifestations are equally dangerous. In my own life, I've gone to both extremes at different times when the ambition inside me has grown distorted. Each of us will naturally lean toward one way or the other, and many leaders will swing back and forth between these two extremes.

AMBITION DISTORTED

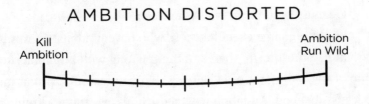

KILL AMBITION

The first response of many leaders, especially Christian leaders, is to look for ways to kill their ambition. If you've been taught to view ambition as a danger to spiritual growth, an impediment to being a follower of Jesus, the spiritual thing to do is to kill it. Because our hearts are naturally deceitful (see Jeremiah 17:9), we cannot trust our desires. Unconstrained ambition may just be a selfish desire. I know many church leaders who struggle with their ambition because they see it as an expression of selfishness or a desire for promotion that might come at the expense of others.

If that's true, what is the easiest and most common way for you to avoid that kind of ambition? You get rid of it! Because we follow the one who said, "If your right eye causes you to stumble, gouge it out" (Matt. 5:29), some leaders take this approach with their ambition—drowning their dreams, abandoning their hopes, and ceasing to pursue more. Why? Because they aren't sure how to channel that desire to lead and bring change into something good and positive. Others may look at that desire and look at their current role and decide that since they haven't been put in charge, they aren't the right one to do anything about it. They've believed the lie we first saw in chapter one: to have influence, you need to be in charge. Since they aren't in a leadership role, they assume the desire is wrong or sinful, a sign of rebellion perhaps.

This is where I was just a few years ago. When I became a campus pastor, I had a lot of ambition for our campus, for our teams, and for myself. I had grand ideas around how we would interact with new guests, what our music culture would feel like, how to bring synergy to the student and children's ministries, and how to create more energy in our adult services. Right or wrong, I felt hamstrung by the structures of authority above me. Without realizing it, the ambition and vision for change I had inside me had grown distorted. So I put it all on mute. I shut it down, thinking that the time wasn't right. It wasn't until that crucial moment in Andy's office that it dawned on me that I wasn't acting wisely or responsibly with my ambition. I was killing it. And killing it is not the answer.

Looking back, I can see where my ambition started moving off course from how we're designed. I was raised in a church where the desire to do something *with* my life was too easily confused with the desire to make something *of* my life. Ambition was outlawed in the name of piety and humility. The people were well-meaning, but the message was clear: kill the ambition before it kills you. When it came to ambition, I thought the rapper Ice Cube said it best: "You better check yo' self before you wreck yo' self."

My senior year of high school, I remember an itinerant preacher rolling through our church, selling a different take on ambition. He told our youth group that we needed to have a "holy ambition." At the time, I thought it was just another weird Christian phrase and a terrible name for a mid-90s Christian boy band. I could imagine the announcement over the PA system at youth group: "Forget Backstreet, 'N Sync, and 98 Degrees! You don't have to go for that, because tonight, we have the latest band to hit the Christian music scene . . . Holy Ambition!" Cue the track. Hit the stage. Crowd goes wild. At least that's how it went in my mind.

I think that preacher was on to something. And while I'm not going to try to sell you on a band called Holy Ambition, the term is useful, especially for a church crowd where any ambition is often too closely associated with the sinful tendency to seek prominence, grab power, and grow in pride at the expense of others. In the church, it's automatically assumed that these three P's are dangerous roommates with ambition, living together in a four-room college suite with an efficiency kitchen. And that association creates confusion for many young leaders. Because there is truth here as well. When our good, God-given ambition is distorted, it can manifest itself in a selfish need to be in charge, to seek recognition, or to exert control over others. Clearly, these distortions of ambition are problematic and flat-out destructive. And that's why so many young leaders, especially those raised in a Christian environment, are too quick to kill their ambition.

To be clear, the New Testament has plain warnings against these distortions of ambition, and they should strike fear in anyone's heart and mind. The New Testament speaks against cultivating ambitions—desires—motivated by selfishness in the pursuit of prominence, pride, and power: "Do nothing out of *selfish ambition* or vain conceit" (Phil. 2:3, emphasis mine) and "For where you have envy and *selfish ambition*, there you find disorder and every evil practice" (James 3:16, emphasis mine).

But these distortions of ambition are just that—distortions. They are rooted in a self-centered desire that masquerades as God-given ambition. Sadly, in the name of holiness and humility, we sometimes take our healthy drive for leadership out back and shoot it, not realizing that drive is actually a gift from God. Without realizing it, we kill the thing that is the very fingerprint of God within us. I'll say more about this later.

So I understand why someone would try to rid him or herself of ambition, but I want to argue that taking the kill shot on your ambition is like throwing the baby out with the bathwater. It's a step too far—a nuclear option that ends up muting any leadership gifts God has given you. Eradicating, abdicating, renouncing, ignoring, or killing the ambition within you is not the answer.

AMBITION RUN WILD

On the flipside, instead of killing their ambitions, some leaders let them run wild. They uncritically embrace them. And we've all seen ambition run wild—it's what those who kill their ambition were trying to avoid. It's the leader who only thinks about himself. The leader who thumbs her nose at the processes and structures and tramples over others without a care for the damage left behind. Some leaders won't go that far, of course. But instead of channeling their ambition in healthy ways, they allow frustration to take control, thinking, *I've got to be in charge and I'll get there by any means necessary.* Or, *I've got to be able to call the shots, or I can't work here.* The extreme of killing ambition focuses on an internal solution to the problem, while the extreme of letting our ambition run wild tends to focus on an external solution. We look to blame others for our lack of authority, we contract a critical spirit toward those who are in charge, and we end up sabotaging the very thing we're seeking. To quote Dr. Phil, "How's that working for ya?"

If you're feeling constrained by those in authority over you right now, you may have picked up this book as a last resort, a solution to your current situation. You may be hoping this book will equip you with the tools you need to work around your boss or to manipulate your boss into doing what you want him or her to do. Maybe this is even a last-ditch effort before you go out and find another job with more opportunity. Or it is the final straw before you go start your own thing, so you can finally lead like you want to lead. If so, I get that. I've felt that way as well. I'm just glad we're talking.

But I also want to say if that's the way you are thinking right now, I need to be clear on this point: leading when you're not in charge *does not* mean you learn skills to get ahead by circumventing the authority above you. Just as the response of killing ambition mutes something God has placed within you, the response of letting your ambition run wild fails by allowing your ambition—instead of God—to take the driver's seat. There is something good in your ambition, to be sure. A leader wants to accomplish something, because that's what is inside of him or her. But then that lie takes root: "I need to be in charge if I want to get anything done." Instead of identifying and removing that lie, we begin to entertain it. Soon we're looking for ways to move our boss out of the way, or trying to work around him or her in an effort to promote our own agenda.

Friends and family can unintentionally fuel this distortion with questions like:

"So when are you going to go out and lead your own thing?"

"When are you going to find a place that appreciates your skills and gives you a bigger position?"

"Your brother is doing such great things in his job. Maybe someday you will as well."

When you hear questions like that, you tend to find affirmation for the hunger you feel to let your ambition run wild—thinking that until you get out from under authority, you can't really do what you're called and gifted to do. You think, *God wants me to lead. I have a mandate to do this. So I need to get the corner office, the reserved parking spot, and the title of senior leader to make that happen.* This kind of ambition just reaffirms the lie that we can't really lead until we're in charge.

Some eager leaders start planning a path to climb the ladder through less than savory means or even by developing an exit plan. We've all seen this distortion leave behind a wake of devastating consequences. These types of leaders will leave an organization too early, bouncing around from job to job, from church to church, hoping to find the golden ticket that allows them to be in charge. Of course, there are leaders who leave for good reasons, after seeking wise counsel and for the good of all involved, and you might need to eventually leave your role as well. Just be aware that you will never find that magical place where you can lead without any constraints. There isn't a healthy church or organization that exists for leaders who think they don't need an authority over them. The dream of an unrestricted frontier where you can lead exactly how you want, when you want, and in the direction you want is a pipe dream. It doesn't exist.

The more leaders I speak with, the more I realize that no one ever feels fully in charge. CEOs answer to boards, principals answer to superintendents, pastors answer to elders, and government officials answer to the people. The idea of a role where you can have all the authority and be fully in charge is found only in a monarchy or a dictatorship.

Leading without constraints and giving into unbridled ambition will be the death of any leader because God didn't intend for our ambition to run wild. I'm not saying you should stick it out in a bad situation forever. You may eventually need to leave your current job. Just know that if you are sensing a voice inside you telling you that your boss is the only obstacle between you and the life you've dreamed of having, it's a distortion of your ambition. You don't need to kill your ambition, but you can't let it run wild. Thankfully, we don't need to follow either extreme. There's another way. A better way.

THE ORIGIN OF AMBITION

I've talked to young leaders who want so badly to be good Christians that they won't allow for any ambition. And I've talked to young leaders who have so much ambition that they don't feel like they can be good Christians. Neither of those is the answer. There is a more Jesus-centered way that allows you to harness the ambition God put in you while remaining where you are.

To understand, we need to go back to the origin of that ambition inside you, the genesis of it all. Understanding your past will always bring more clarity for your future. So we need to understand *what* ambition is, *where* it comes from, *why* God has put it in you, and *how* to harness it for the purpose it was given.

In the creation account of Genesis 1, we read about how God made us: "So God created mankind in his own image, in the image of God he created them; male and female he created them" (Gen. 1:27). You and I were made in God's image. The *imago dei*. We were stamped with the image of God, and that has been passed down to us from generation to generation from the beginning of time. If you haven't processed the weight of that, now would be a great time. *When God made you, he had himself in mind.*

I've had the beautiful and unforgettable moments of holding each of our kids for the first time. And at different times and in different forms, this verse from Genesis has inevitably popped into my head. I think about how this little delight, this bundle of joy I'm holding, was formed in the image of God. This child was fashioned, designed, formed, and shaped in the image of the Creator, giving them the highest possible value. And the same is true of you and me. If imitation is the highest form of flattery, this truth speaks directly to our value. You are most valuable because you were created to be like your Creator.

When God created the world, he attributed the highest honor to humankind by creating us in his likeness, with his characteristics, and imbued with his purposes. Tucked in the middle of this beautiful act, God named the purpose for which he created us. In the next verse, God gave two actions of purpose. "God blessed them and said to them, '*Be fruitful* and *increase* in number'" (Gen. 1:28, emphasis mine).

God blesses us by giving us a purpose for living. He gives us an agency—something to do. First, he says, "Be fruitful and increase in number." That's the fun part! All kidding aside . . . let me be the first to say there's very little that is more annoying than pastors who incessantly make sex jokes. It's always slightly disturbing to me, so I'll spare you the ones that immediately come to mind here. What is important is that we see the drive to "be fruitful and increase in number" as both a *gift* and a *responsibility* to steward.

Let me add that you should certainly have "the birds and the bees" talk with your kids, but they're probably going to figure it out eventually, because it's hardwired into them. But just because they have it doesn't mean they will see *why* God gave it. They need help understanding why it is given and what God intends us to do with it. God clearly gave us this drive, but he also gave us a context for this drive. In the same way that trying to kill ambition isn't a great option, trying to kill that desire to "be fruitful and increase in number" doesn't work either. That's why Paul comes along in 1 Corinthians 7 and says to get married if trying to kill the sex drive is killing you. If you leave the drive to "be fruitful and increase in number" unchecked and let it run wild, it will bring negative consequences. The classic image we give to students in our ministry is that "fire outside the fireplace is dangerous." God gave us a context for the drive he gave us, so we must discover the context and harness it for good. Sex is a fantastic gift and it shouldn't be ignored. Letting it run wild leads to all kinds of trouble in this life, but suppressing it, ignoring it, and treating it like a curse is also a big mistake.

Sex isn't the focus of this book, but I've been talking about it because what's true for that God-given purpose is equally true for the next one we see in Genesis 1:28 (emphasis mine): "God blessed them and said to them, 'Be fruitful and increase in number; fill the earth and *subdue* it.'" This command to "subdue it" is a mandate for leadership, and in this mandate, we find a clue to the third option I've been talking about—that middle way that helps us understand what we should do with the ambition God has put inside us.

The Hebrew verb that we translate in English as *subdue* has a greater depth and meaning than our English translation captures. To fully understand the intent behind the command, we have to remember the context in which God spoke this. So where were Adam and Eve? They were where God had put them when he made them—in a garden. If we want to grasp this mandate, the context of the garden of Eden has to be front and center in our minds.

SPACE TO GROW

Every March, I'm giddy as an eager little puppy at the thought of planting vegetables. Whether it's the turn of the weather, the activity it provides our kids, or the temptation I feel as I see the ads at the hardware store, I just can't not want to garden. I'm not saying I'm good at it. My thumb, as it turns out, is not that green. My wife, Jenny, gets quite frustrated with me because she sees my gardening attempts as a complete waste of money. Last year, as the weather started to get warmer, she said to me, "Instead of wasting your time on that garden, why don't you just skip the work and donate $100 to Home Depot?" I'm crying inside as I type this.

For whatever reason, something inside me comes alive when I find the right soil combination and get my hands dirty working that soil. The sight of a seed I've planted sprouting out of the ground is thrilling, and that moment when something is ripe enough to be plucked off the vine makes me feel like a boss! Last year, I had one pepper that survived my gardening efforts and I paraded it around the kitchen like LeBron in Cleveland with his championship trophy.

You can tell that I am not the best gardener, because I threw a celebration over one small pepper. But as terrible as I am, I'm slowly learning what it takes for these delicious little veggie nuggets to grow. I'm learning how to subdue the elements so they work together to grow something. I'm learning how to subdue water for the benefit of the plants. I'm learning how to subdue the ground to give the cucumbers enough space to flourish. I'm learning to plant at just the right location to subdue the sunlight for the benefit of the herbs. I'm learning to plant marigolds around the bed to subdue the deer so they do not eat the strawberries. I'm bringing the elements God has provided under my control for the benefit of the little veggies I'm serving, so they have what they need to grow, develop, and become what they're meant to become. The work of subduing these elements to produce a fruitful result in gardening is a great metaphor for the God-given drive toward leadership that was placed within us at the beginning of time. Here's why.

The mandate to *subdue* is something deep within me, and it's deep within you as well. But just because it's in me doesn't mean I'm always handling it well and directing it wisely. Just because it's deep within me doesn't mean it's going to come out of me in the way God intended. And the same is true for you. We all have it, but there's always the potential for it to be twisted, perverted, and co-opted.

FINDING KABASH

While I didn't "Doogie Howser" seminary, I enjoyed it, but I'm still very aware that I'm a practitioner and not a scholar. I took the standard four semesters of Hebrew, but I'm not an expert. I can still interpret Hebrew well enough to know that the Hebrew word for "subdue" is an interesting one. In Hebrew, it looks like this: כָּבַשׁ

If you were to pronounce this word, reading from right to left as the Hebrew language does, it would create the sound kā·băš or *kavash* or *kabash*. If you don't spit on the pages of this book when you hit that "k," you haven't hit it hard enough. Go ahead. Give it a whirl. I find that saying it out loud is like eating a bag of Funyuns. It's not all that good for you, but it's hard to stop, because it's just so dang fun.

As I started playing around with that word on my tongue, sounding it out, it sounded strangely familiar to me. Does it sound familiar to you too? It reminded me of that English phrase we sometimes use—the word "kibosh." As in "put the kibosh on that thing," or in other words—stop it. End it. It's over. Done.

There aren't many shows that make me laugh like *Seinfeld*. If you don't consider it one of the greatest sitcoms of all time, we'll have trouble being friends. Through years and years of mental training, I have conditioned my mind to operate on two levels: on one level, I function in life. On another level, I run my life through my "*Seinfeld* Directory," making connections between my life and various *Seinfeld* episodes. It's taken years of what some would say has been wasted time and effort, but deep down it brings me joy. And that makes it worth it to me.

In the ninth episode of season four, in a show titled "The

Opera," "Crazy" Joe Davola leaves Jerry a fantastic message on his answering machine, laced with the word "kibosh."

> Jerry, Joe Davola. (*Joe starts spitting) I have a hair on my tongue. Can't get it off. (*Still spitting) You know how much I hate that? Of course you do. You put it there.
>
> I know what you said about me, Seinfeld. I know you bad-mouthed me to the execs at NBC—put the kibosh on my deal. Now I'm gonna put the kibosh on you. You know I've kiboshed before. And I will kibosh again.[1]

If you have a few minutes and can handle this kind of distraction, you should do yourself a favor and YouTube this clip. I guarantee it will bring you thirty-seven seconds of chuckles and an immeasurable amount of lingering giggles.

The word Joe Davola uses, *kibosh*, is eerily similar to that Hebrew word we saw in Genesis, *kabash*. Note that for the sake of clarity, I'm going to spell these words differently, but I should add that the more I study the creation mandate in Genesis 1:28, the more convinced I am that *kibosh* in the *Seinfeld* sense is somehow a derivative of the *kabash* of Genesis. Full disclosure: I've searched and searched to find the etymology of the word *kibosh*, but in the end it's just not clear that the two are connected. No one really knows where the word came from. But even though there is no clear pathway from *kibosh* back to *kabash*, I'm convinced these two words must be kinfolk—cousins, if you will.[2]

They sound alike and may even be related, but they've come to mean very different things.

Kabash /'kä bäSH/
to subdue, cultivate, and organize something in such a way that it thrives, grows, and flourishes
"fill the earth and subdue it."

Kibosh /'kī bäSH/

to put an end to something or to dispose of it decisively
"put the *kibosh* on my deal"

Kabash, as we first see it in Genesis, speaks to the ambition God has given us to lead—our drive to subdue, cultivate, and organize so this world flourishes. It's a good thing, a gift we need to steward creatively and responsibly. But here's the problem: far too often, that good *kabash* becomes *kibosh*—an attitude of opposition and negativity that kills creativity and shirks responsibility. When we give in to *kibosh*, we are embracing a distortion of *kabash*. I'm convinced that we've taken God's good command in Genesis 1 and twisted it. It may not be intentional, but somehow we've taken God's command to *kabash* and have filled it with a new meaning—the exact opposite of what God intended.

THE KIBOSH LEADER

I use these two words—*kibosh* and *kabash*—as a shorthand way of thinking about two different kinds of leaders and two different ways to respond to ambition. You've probably experienced the *kibosh* type of leader. Jesus referred to this kind of leader. He gave us a picture of what this looks like in others and warned us against following in the same way. In Mark 10, Jesus's closest followers were arguing over who was going to have the title and the position required to be the leader once Jesus was gone. Without rebuking their desire to lead, Jesus quickly and sharply rebuked their misguided views on leadership. "Jesus called them together and said, 'You know that those who are regarded as rulers of the Gentiles lord it over them, and their high officials exercise

79

authority over them'" (Mark 10:42). The *kibosh* leaders are the ones that lord their authority over those entrusted to them. The *kibosh* leaders leverage authority not to serve others, but to serve themselves. Let's revisit our diagram of Ambition Distorted and see how it relates to the *kibosh* leader.

AMBITION DISTORTED

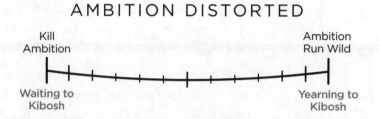

We saw earlier that there are two ways we distort our God-given ambition. Some of us, when we're not in charge, resort to waiting until we're in charge to step out and lead. We pass the buck and just do what's asked of us. When we believe the lie that authority is required to lead, that good desire to *kabash*—to embrace the creativity and responsibility God has placed within us—gets co-opted into *kibosh*—a selfish negativity toward anything that doesn't benefit us directly.

The simple answer for how *kabash* became *kibosh* is sin. When Adam and Eve disobeyed God, sin entered the world and distorted everything, including the good ambition God placed within us, that desire to make something great or achieve something of worth. Adam and Eve's fatal decision was to believe too little of God and too much of themselves. God gave them full dominion to *kabash* all his creation, but he gave them one stipulation—do not eat from the Tree of the Knowledge of Good and Evil. For whatever reason, they didn't believe he was to be trusted, and they disobeyed. This act set in motion the evolution of *kabash* to *kibosh,* from responsible stewardship of our ambition for God's glory into a selfish negativity that seeks only what is best for me and mine.

The desire to rule or control without restraint is dangerous, but so is the inner passivity of waiting to have authority in order to lead. We might fall into the trap of believing it's up to us—if it's going to get done, we must do it at whatever cost, regardless of those in authority over us. This extreme doesn't operate in faith and reliance on God but trusts in our own abilities *apart* from God. There are many who fall into the opposite trap—thinking we need to wait around until God gives us a certain title or promotion. But God doesn't want us to sit back. He wants us to responsibly engage, doing the work he has given us wherever we are, with whatever title or role he has currently assigned to us.

The lie of *kibosh* is that God can't be trusted, so I need to passively wait or take matters into my own hands. But the truth of *kabash* is that God has given us ambition, and when I responsibly cultivate that ambition and gain influence by answering his call upon my life, I'll eventually have the authority to do what he wants me to do. That's what separates *kibosh* leaders from *kabash* leaders. Great leaders, young and old, understand that God is the one who gives authority and that having influence is the path toward authority, not the other way around. As we learn to trust that God is the one to establish authority, we find ourselves becoming the *kabash* leaders God intended us to be.

Let's review:

- You have ambition because you were created with the drive to create, contribute, and influence things around you. We saw that killing that ambition *or* letting it run wild will create negative consequences.

- In Genesis, God names the ambition inside you and calls it *kabash*. To *kabash* is to bring something under your control so you can make it more effective, beautiful, and useful.
- Over time, the *kabash* God has given you has been co-opted by sin into *kibosh*. To *kibosh* is to bring something under your control for your own good through dominant authority.
- When your *kibosh* is passive, it leaves you waiting on authority to lead, abdicating your responsibility as someone created in God's image. When *kibosh* is active, though, it manifests as selfish ambition where you are working for self-advancement and the ability to control others for your own purposes.

THE KABASH LEADER

God wants us to live out the *kabash* he's put in us, exercising it under his authority and for his glory. Instead of waiting for the authority to lead or working in selfish ways to see that authority for our own ends, he wants us to resist *kibosh* and reclaim *kabash*. This is the path toward true leadership.

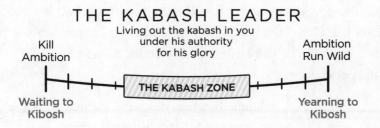

The older I get, the more I realize that between the extremes there is usually a third option. We grow up thinking life is black and white. As a father of four, I know the brains of the little ones in our home have yet to develop the capability of understanding the nuances of life. When we are young, we need authority figures to give us direction on what is right and wrong. But at some point, we have to train our minds to resist simplistic and dualistic thinking. As we grow in wisdom and discernment, we usually find there is a third option, a middle way that better captures the realities of life.

Jesus did this all the time. The teachers of the law were constantly trying to catch him in black or white, yes or no, good or bad scenarios, but he transcended their elementary thinking with a third option that shattered their categories. For instance, in Mark 12, the Pharisees are found trying to trap Jesus with binary options, but he offers them a third way. "Give back to Caesar what is Caesar's and to God what is God's" (Mark 12:17).

To this day, Jesus gives us all a way forward. His way allows us to love people in messy situations while also striving for the righteousness he desires for us. His way allows us to find contentment in our circumstances and also drives us to make the world better. His way brings the fullness of truth with the fullness of grace. In his teachings, Jesus presents us with a third way that honors God, a way in-between the two extremes of our sin.

A *kabash* leader doesn't need authority, but he or she cultivates influence through relationships. A *kabash* leader knows that the way to the front isn't by pushing ahead or waiting until the game is over; it's getting behind people and helping them move ahead. Just like a master gardener, a *kabash* leader gives space for people to thrive and cultivates growth in others through time, attention, care, and kind correction. The way to lead is to serve, and the way to create something great is to give people space to thrive in the way God has gifted each one. A *kabash* leader is marked with humility because they know that pride sets us against God (see James 4:6). A *kabash* leader is courageous, not because they possess inner strength, but because they know God is the one who controls the destiny of every man and woman. A *kabash* leader longs to organize and create for the betterment of all—for the good of others and not just the good of the leader. A *kabash* leader uses his or her influence to help others get ahead and not to get ahead of others. A *kabash* leader pours out, trusting that God's new mercies each day will be enough to fill them up.

Rather than killing the ambition within you, that God-given desire to create, I want to encourage you to find the third way of the *kabash* leader. It's more powerful than a title and more influential than a position. It's the way God originally designed you to lead.

AMBITION TO GLORIFY GOD

The true test of the *kabash* leader is found in his or her motivation. So as you dig into your ambition and unpack your motives for leading, you'll better understand why you desire to be a leader in the first place. To lead like you were designed to lead, you must weigh your heart and your desires. Are you in this for yourself or for others? Each of us must answer the question: for whom am I living? As a leader, you can ask it this way: for whom am I *leading*? *Kabash* leaders understand that the motive for leadership is to help others for God's glory.

When one of the experts in the law asked Jesus about the greatest commandment, he cut through the clutter and confusion of that question and offered a hauntingly clear answer. Jesus doesn't specifically mention God's glory here, but I believe that in answering the question of what is most fundamental in what God expects from us, he is giving us a practical guide to what we can do to bring God the utmost glory and honor. Jesus replied, "'Love the Lord your God with all your heart and with all your soul and with all your mind.' This is the first and greatest commandment. And the second is like it: 'Love your neighbor as yourself'" (Matt. 22:37–38).

Jesus tells us that the greatest commandment is to love God. That's the most God-glorifying thing I can think of! But he follows that with a second command, which is also clear. What he says is that for us to fully live out the *kabash* God has put in us, in a way that shows love for him, it must also be for the benefit of others—and not for us alone. When a person attempts to *kabash* for their own glory, they end up putting the *kibosh* on everyone else.

If you picked up this book because you're hoping it will be the roadmap to finding your next big thing, you're welcome to go ahead and set it down. If you're hoping this book will offer some nice tips that will help you build your own kingdom, you're going to be disappointed. I can't help you with that. But if your hands are open to whatever God might want to do through you, even if that means you'll never be in charge, I think I can help. Because when the *kabash* in you is harnessed under God's authority and for his glory, you'll find yourself leading in the way you were meant to lead. And I think that's worth as much time as you're willing to spend.

PART 2

The Four
Behaviors

CHAPTER 4

LEAD
YOURSELF

No man or woman is ever fully acquitted of all responsibility. Just as there are inalienable rights, there is such a thing as inalienable responsibility. What this means is that *everyone* leads something. Everyone is *in charge* of something—even if it's just you. Each one of us is responsible for the choices and decisions we make. We must all learn to rightly influence ourselves.

For people currently working under the authority of someone else, someone they must answer to, what do you think is the number one excuse for failure to do a job well? Here are some clues: It's one word. It's a person. And it rhymes with "sauce."

When most people think about the challenges of leading when they aren't in charge, the most common excuse they give for their failure is—you guessed it—their *boss*.

- "My boss would never go for that. She hardly even listens to my ideas."
- "My boss is just not willing to change. He's not even open to a conversation about it."
- "I'm so frustrated because my boss is so stuck in the past. I mean, she will listen but never does anything with it."

It's likely that, at some point, we'll all have to work for a bad leader, but that is not an excuse. I say that even though I don't know your situation. I realize there are some bosses who are insecure, unaware, and defensive and are intimidated if you choose to exercise any kind of leadership when you're not yet in charge. What I'm going to say in this chapter may feel next to impossible. But let me ask you: what is the chance there is still something you can learn in this situation where you currently find yourself? Even if that chance is one in a million, I'd like to quote my friend and yours, Lloyd Christmas, "So you're telling me there's a chance. Yeah!"

When you aren't accomplishing what you want to accomplish in the role you're in, it's natural to look for someone to blame. And the easiest target is your boss, especially when you've already concluded he or she is a bad leader. When you make a judgment about someone, specifically your manager, you will persistently look for behaviors to justify the judgment you've made. Then, with your settled judgment in place, you look for every possible reason no one else would or could succeed in your role. It's a self-defeating prophecy where you give yourself a pass for your own lack of leadership.

THE HALL PASS

Do you remember asking for the "hall pass" in high school? I do. Vividly. In tenth-grade US history class, Mr. Truhett had a laminated picture of Han Solo and Chewbacca that read, "Hall Pass: It's dangerous to go Solo! Take a Wookie with you." That still cracks me up! If you were able to get your paws on that hall pass, you could wander the halls, peeking into every other class in the school to find someone to make eye contact with and hopefully distract them. If someone tried to stop you, you just held up Han Solo and Chewy—hall pass!

The hall pass is a dangerous thing. In school, the hall pass excused any type of behavior. You could be doing whatever you wanted in the hall, and if you held up that pass, you had an out. However, the hall pass does not help us in the end. The hall pass is nice in the moment, but it keeps us from learning things in the classroom that we really need to learn. It keeps us from experiencing what we need to experience to grow. All of us need to be cautious using the "hall pass" in leadership as well.

If you want to grow as a leader, please resist the temptation to use the "hall pass" of having a bad manager. Even if you're working for a bad leader, at the very least, you can use this opportunity to learn how to avoid becoming the leader you despise when others are working for you in the future. At the end of this chapter, I will offer some thoughts that may be helpful for you. You may be facing one of the toughest questions a growing leader who is not in charge faces: when working for a bad leader, at what point is it time to cut bait and move on? Until then, I want to convince you of a powerful truth that we all need to learn before we go about blaming our managers and excusing ourselves from our God-given call to lead.

WHERE THE BUCK STOPS

Here's the truth you need to know: *Your boss is not in charge of you. You are in charge of you.*

A few years ago, our humorous son, Jake, came home from preschool and dropped a truth-bomb in our kitchen—one that is still reverberating in my ears today. It was around 5:00 p.m., and I had just walked in the house from work.

I asked him, "Hey buddy, how was school?"

He answered, "Good." After all, he's a male. What else is he supposed to say?

He then went on to offer a little more detail. "Hey Daddy, you know what?"

"No, I don't. What's up?"

"I'm in charge of me."

Instinctively, I cut my eyes at my wife. My look basically said, "Who is teaching him this garbage?"

Jenny went on to explain that Jake's preschool teacher makes a huge deal out of that statement. Jake's teacher cannot make Jake pick up his toys after he's finished playing with them. She cannot force Jake to eat his food. She cannot keep Jake from hitting Will for calling him a "chicken nugget." And I had to admit that she's right. Jake is in charge of Jake.

I have recalled that conversation so many times because the implication of that truth is so powerful for every one of us. It's not just true for three-year-olds; it's true for thirty-one-year-olds. You are in charge of you. You are in charge of your emotions, your thoughts, your reactions, and your decisions. It's the law of personal responsibility, because everyone is responsible for leading something, even if that something is just you.

When you're not in charge, the most common temptation you'll face is to abdicate responsibility. "If they had wanted me to take responsibility, they would have put me in charge. And since I'm not in charge of everything, I'm in charge of nothing." But this is dangerous. This attitude is not evidence of a lack of leadership; it's a sign of *bad* leadership. Remember, we're all leaders.

You have leadership in you, and if you find yourself abdicating responsibility because you're not in charge, step one is to recognize it. Step two is to fix it. And that leads us to the second truth you need to know as a leader: *When you're not in charge, you can still take charge.*

To put this in the form of an Old English question, "Of what should you take charge?" Great question. For starters, the answer is you. You should take charge of you.

MISPLACED EXPECTATIONS

Too often, I hear younger leaders in our organization say, "I'm just so frustrated because I can't find anyone to pour into me." This drives me bananas. I'd rather have my head sewn to the carpet than hear someone complain, "I can't find someone to pour into me." If you're not being led well, don't pass the buck. Maybe, just maybe, the reason you're not being led well is that you're not leading yourself well. Before you go and blame your manager, try applying the wisdom of the King of Pop: "I'm starting with the man in the mirror. I'm asking him to change his ways."[1] Personally, I can't read those lyrics without singing in my head.

The point is that your greatest responsibility as a leader is to lead yourself. MJ didn't have everything right, but I think he had this right. If you want to see change, begin with the person in the mirror.

One of my least favorite conversations in the church revolves around the concept of "going deeper." Every few months, someone approaches me in the lobby after one of our services. They begin by telling me that I look like I've lost weight. I try not to spill the sarcasm everywhere, so I respond, "Well, thank you, but no, I have not. Now, you seem to have a complaint. What concerns you?"

That's when they drop the bomb. "Clay, I just . . . I just don't feel like we're going deep enough." Hmmm. Are we at scuba class or are we at church? I'm a bit confused. Have you ever heard that before? "We're not going deep enough." The correct response in this situation is a Christian moo. "Hmmmmm. Tell me more."

I try to have them clarify what they mean. Typically, I'll ask, "What do you mean by 'going deep'?" And they say, "Well, I wish we could do a deep dive through the Old Testament."

So then I go, "Okay, that's fantastic. I've spent a lot of years in seminary, so if you want to do a deep dive through the Old Testament, we could do that. Let me ask you a question first, though. Have you started reading the Old Testament for yourself?"

They always seem to be offended when I ask this, with a look that says, "What does that have to do with anything?"

Well, what does that have to do with anything? Great question. That has everything to do with anything. Why? Because if you lack the drive to start reading the Old Testament yourself, how in the world do you expect someone else to take you on a deep dive through it? Before others can lead you, you must learn to lead yourself. You need to own your desires and ambitions; no one can lead you any further than you're leading yourself. Have you experienced the frustration of trying to lead someone who is not leading him or herself well? A teenager, perhaps? It's maddening. As the adage says, "I would much rather steer racehorses than carry racehorses."

Steering a racehorse is exhilarating.

Carrying a racehorse is exhausting.

It's easy to blame someone for not leading you well. Resist that urge, own your ambition, and begin to lead yourself.

FAITHFUL WITH LITTLE

I've come close to having this quote by Tom Watson, former IBM CEO, tattooed on my body. (Though that would be super weird, I'm sure.) "Nothing so conclusively proves a man's ability to lead others as what he does on a day-to-day basis to lead himself."[2]

We live in a time where anyone, at any age, from anywhere in the world, can become famous. Have you noticed that? It's kind of amazing. I love it and hate it at the same time. From "eyebrows on fleek" to Antoine Dodson of "Hide ya kids" fame or the guy who won a talent show by flipping a water bottle a single revolution and landing it perfectly on a table, instant fame always feels like it is right around the corner. Any one of us is just one post away from going viral and landing ourselves on the *Weekend Update* on *Saturday Night Live.* That's pretty cool. And pretty scary.

One thing that is not going viral is what you're doing to lead yourself. I say this because it's not sexy. It's not newsworthy. It might not even be noteworthy, but it's definitely worthwhile. It's the discipline of the little things. Every time you're on time, every time you tell someone you're going to email a file and you follow through, every time you read something for your betterment, every time you finish a workout or a class, every single time you say no to the impulse buy at Costco, you're exercising something that will never go viral but is incredibly significant.

Jesus was making a statement about stewardship when he said, "Whoever can be trusted with very little can also be trusted with much" (Luke 16:10), but implicit in what he's saying is that there's so much more at stake in how you're leading yourself than just you leading yourself. With the small choices you make when no one else is looking, when it's just you and God, you are proving or disproving to him (and to yourself) your future ability to lead others. When a younger leader tells me he is frustrated at not having a voice yet or not having influence yet, the answer I give him is to continue to be faithful in leading himself well. You can never go wrong by making that decision.

THE GAME PLAN

So what does that look like, practically? It requires three simple things. I'll never forget Dr. Howard Hendricks telling our seminary class, "If you think this is too simple, remember that Jesus said, 'Feed my sheep' not 'Feed my giraffes.'" So while these three things are simple, I don't think they are simplistic. They're easy enough to grasp, but will take a lifetime to master.

Self-Leadership Principle #1: Model Followership.

If you want to lead well when you are not the one in charge, it's imperative that you learn how to *model followership*. What do I mean? Do you know how to follow well? Does the team around you know that you're following well? Would they say, "Oh yeah, she's fully behind the leader" or "Yes, definitely. He's 100 percent behind his leader"? The water cooler talk and office gossip cannot be a part of your life if you're going to do this right. In an attempt to connect with coworkers or even put yourself ahead, belittling your boss through needless chatter actually hurts you more than it hurts him or her. Your moral authority is vastly more important than your positional authority, and nothing erodes moral authority more than undermining the person you claim to be following.

So the first step to master in becoming a leader who leads well when not in charge is how to model what it means to be a follower. As others see how you respond to a bad boss, a terrible decision, or how you handle the stress of being overloaded, they will begin to see you as a leader, even if you lack the formal authority to lead. Your self-leadership in these situations will develop influence and prepare you for future situations you may face.

Self-Leadership Principle #2: Monitor Your Heart and Behavior.

What is easier to monitor, your heart or your behavior? The truth is that they're both difficult. The feelings and emotions in our hearts are invisible and difficult to see in the mirror. But our behaviors also have the potential to betray us. All of us have behaved in ways we didn't want to behave or failed to act on something we wanted to act on. Monitoring your heart involves checking those deep-rooted motives and emotions that lie inside you and give direction to your behaviors. With just a bit of curiosity and initiative, our behaviors may initially be easier to identify.

Monitoring your heart requires constantly checking your motives and feelings before God. There is good reason David is called "a man after God's own heart." Look at all the times in Psalms when he bared his soul before God, begging God to help him keep his heart pure.

How can a young person stay on the path of purity?
By living according to your word.
PSALM 119:9

Test me, LORD, and try me,
examine my heart and my mind.
PSALM 26:2

Search me, God, and know my heart;
test me and know my anxious thoughts.
See if there is any offensive way in me,
and lead me in the way everlasting.
PSALM 139:23–24

No one can do this for you. You have to make a decision to constantly check the emotions of your heart. Has any jealousy rooted itself in your heart? Is someone getting attention you feel you deserve? Do you feel anger toward your boss for something that has happened in the past? Are you frustrated about getting passed over for a promotion or more responsibility? Leading ourselves requires monitoring those dark corners of our hearts where these dangerous emotions lie. Monitoring your behavior must be both horizontal (with others) and vertical (with God). This will mean asking some tough questions of those around you.

A few years ago, I made a pretty significant job transition. During that transition, someone recommended I read *The First 90 Days: Proven Strategies for Getting Up to Speed Faster and Smarter.*[5] I did, and it was fantastically helpful. One recommendation the author, Michael Watkins, makes is to solicit as much feedback as possible from your old job before jumping directly into your new job. I was reading this at just the right time. Without his advice to assess my vulnerabilities, I would have jumped right into my new role because I was so eager for the new responsibility. Instead, I submitted an informal, anonymous 360-degree survey to about fifty of the coworkers I had in my former role. I asked them three simple questions:

1. What did I do over the past few years that inspired you?
2. What did I do that frustrated you?
3. What do I not know about myself that has become a blind spot?

I received a lot of positive feedback. Unfortunately, I don't remember any of that. I just remember a few comments, which have caused significant changes in the way I operate at work.

"At times, I felt like you weren't really paying attention to me, but were only thinking about what you had next."

"Sometimes when I'm around you, I get the sense that you don't really want to hear what I have to say because you've already made up your mind."

"When we would meet together, you never really seemed prepared for our meeting."

These comments were invaluable, but they were not news to me. None of them shocked me. I already knew some of this about myself. I was just hoping no one else knew it too.

A healthy curiosity should drive your efforts to monitor your behavior. And not just curiosity for curiosity's sake, but curiosity for the sake of growth. You need to cultivate interest in how others see the way you act and lead. There is feedback orbiting around your world that could change you, grow you, stretch you, and make you better, but the responsibility for soliciting that feedback is yours! You are in charge of you!

Self-Leadership Principle #3: Make a Plan.

To lead yourself well, you need a plan. You will not lead yourself well by accident. It must be intentional. I call it a "Lead Me Plan." Everyone needs to be able to answer this question: what are you doing to lead yourself well? What is your "Lead Me Plan"? To lead you well, you need to focus on three simple aspects:

1. Know where you currently are.
2. Have a vision for where you want to go.
3. Develop the discipline and accountability to do what it takes to stay on track.

KNOW WHERE YOU ARE

As you are developing a "Lead Me Plan," the greatest mistake you can make is to inflate your own leadership ability. You have gifts, talents, experience, and education that got you where you are. Don't try to fool yourself. You haven't arrived! What got you there will not get you where you want to be.

Jim Collins noted this mistake made by some successful leaders and companies in *How the Mighty Fall: And Why Some Companies Never Give In*. He called it "the hubris of success." The first misstep success brings is to credit the success to your own doing, but this only sets leaders up for future failure: "Truly great [leaders], no matter how successful they become, maintain a learning curve as steep as when they first began their careers."[4] For you to maintain a steep learning curve in this season of your life, you'll need to be honest about where you are and how you got there. This kind of gut-level assessment of where you are will only happen by asking for it. People around you love you. They really do. They want you to get better. They want you to grow.

But rarely will someone love you enough to give you the full truth. I see people walking around with untied shoes, susceptible to tripping, and no one around them is courageous enough to tell them. If you want to know where you are and how you're doing, you have to ask.

One of our key leadership roles recently opened up, and we started talking about who we were going to hire for that position. During the conversation, someone brought up two names of people inside our organization who were interested in the job. The problem was that they had some pretty big gaps in their leadership skills that would keep them from being considered for the job. I asked the person who manages them if the employees were aware of these gaps that were keeping them from being considered. The answer I received was inconclusive, and that frustrated me for their sakes. We won't improve unless someone is honest with us.

Most of the big employment decisions in your career will happen when you're not in the room. That's sobering, but I know it's been true for my career. I've gotten jobs and I've lost jobs based on what people have said about me in rooms where I was not present. At times, some have spoken positively about me, and at other times, some have spoken negatively about me. Either way, it's their opinion of me that matters. The same is true about your career. The people you work for have thoughts about you. They may even have thoughts about your future. It doesn't help you if there is something keeping you from an opportunity—but you are the only one who doesn't know it.

Before you put a plan together for your own growth, you should ask your boss a question: "If an opportunity for promotion came available, what would keep you from fully recommending me?" The answer to that question could be the genesis for your personal growth plan. A word of advice on this: I wouldn't ambush your boss with that question. Send him an email to tee it up, and mention that you would like to ask him some questions to help you in your job performance. Then follow up in person. And be aware that most people will resist answering that question because it is difficult to answer. Still, the feedback you receive is a good place to start. Follow it up with input from others as well.

WHERE YOU WANT TO GO

Once you know where you are, the next step is to develop a clear vision for where you want to go. This is often overlooked when people work on a "Lead Me Plan." One of my weaknesses as a leader is vision—both personally and professionally. I am much more comfortable responding to opportunities rather than looking down the road a few years and imagining my future.

A few years ago, my boss approached me with a potential promotion. I called my good friend Bryson to tell him the news. His response bewildered me. In fact, his response was no response. I had to repeat myself because I thought maybe he hadn't heard me. After telling him again, there was no response. So I had to ask him, "What do you think about that?" I fully expected him to say, "Wow. That's so great! Congrats, dude." It seemed appropriate.

Instead, he said, "Man, I've gotta be honest. I don't know whether to say 'congrats' or 'sorry.' I just don't know what you want, so I don't know what to say. It feels like they're just yanking you around without giving you a say. Just seems like you need to figure out what you want to do with your life before I know how to respond."

We all need friends like that. We need friends who remind us that we aren't just responding to opportunities and circumstances. We each need to have a personal vision for our own lives, a plan for our futures. Without a personal vision for your life, how do you know what to do with the opportunities that present themselves? Especially the good ones, like a promotion?

Self-leadership means spending the necessary time and effort to determine your own personal vision for your future. I see many young leaders who have no clear sense of direction, and that can be paralyzing. And while people will probably tell you that your plan for your life rarely works out the way you think it will, aiming at nothing will take you nowhere. It's dangerous to hold too tightly to the plans we've determined for ourselves, but it's just as dangerous to have no vision or direction for stewarding the gifts, talents, and opportunities God has given us.

There are a few questions that have helped me zero in on how to respond to what God has put in front of me.

- If money were no issue, what would I choose to do with my time?
- What really bothers me? What breaks my heart?
- What makes me pound the table in frustration or passion?
- What gives me life or makes me come alive?

Spend time answering these questions with other people that know you well. It's one of the most crucial ingredients to leading yourself well.

DISCIPLINE AND ACCOUNTABILITY

If God told you that you could ask him for anything you wanted and the answer would be yes, what would you ask for? That's a pretty thrilling thought. Because we have little kids, we play this question out in our homes pretty often. The ability to fly is the most popular answer my kids give. But the ability to generate ice cream at any point and at any time is clearly the correct answer.

In all seriousness, I would ask for more self-discipline to accomplish the tasks I want to accomplish and to be the person I want to be. I say that because without the self-discipline necessary to see a "Lead Me Plan" through, it's an empty plan. The good news is that I believe everyone has a motivating factor that will help spur on the self-discipline necessary to see the "Lead Me Plan" through to the end.

What motivates you? What creates accountability to help you learn, grow, and stretch yourself in ways you wouldn't otherwise? If you're driven by achievement, sign up for a class at a school or some type of certification program. Most of us aren't in it for the certificate, but it's a form of self-discipline. For me, the implicit accountability with the school is great motivation. I wish I would read and write on my own time, but I need some accountability. So paying tuition motivates me to complete the tasks assigned on the syllabus.

If you're relational, maybe you need to create a group of your peers to learn and grow together. This is the idea behind book reading groups. There is built-in accountability to read, form opinions, and show up to the group. You'll end up doing work and thinking about what you're reading in ways you wouldn't have normally done. Even better, offer to lead the group. Taking on the responsibility to lead will force you to think through things you normally would not. You'll need to take initiative and ask different questions.

If you're wired for order and routine, determine a plan and tell someone about it. Or hire a coach who will help you formulate a plan. This works well in the realm of physical fitness, and the growing trend of CrossFit groups and fitness boot camps highlights this. People pay good money for someone to choose a fitness plan for them, set a time for them to show up, and provide the community of people that will push them along. And we don't just need this physically; we need this in all areas of our lives.

If you just lack motivation, pick a goal, set a deadline, and create an artificial consequence to motivate you. I'm convinced this is why people run marathons. Think about it. You're paying money to show up early on a Saturday morning to inflict pain on your body. Why? I ask people that all the time. The answer never makes sense to me. "Because it's fun!" Not for me. Sounds like hell. Literally. All that being said, a deadline and an artificial consequence are quite motivating and might just be what you need to kick-start your self-leadership.

I know I need to grow in how I handle conflict. More specifically, I need to grow in my ability to deal with tense, high-stakes conversations. Part of my "Lead Me Plan" is to read two books, *Crucial Conversations*[5] and *Difficult Conversations*,[6] and then give a leadership talk on this topic to a few friends at work. Without this kind of self-imposed discipline and accountability, I just wouldn't do it. The date of the talk is on the calendar. I know people will show up. And the accountability even makes me nervous as I type this. But that's the point. A "Lead Me Plan" must also build in means of pressure and systems of accountability to help execute it.

At the beginning of this year, I created a simple chart for my current "Lead Me Plan." It's not complicated, and you're welcome to use this one or create your own. The point is to have a plan. If someone were to ask you what your future plan is, what you're doing to lead yourself should be top of mind. If you don't have an answer when someone asks you, you don't really have a plan.

LEAD ME PLAN	WHERE AM I?	OBJECTIVES	EXECUTION & ACCOUNTABILITY
Self-Health	Complaints of being distracted in one-on-one meetings	Be more present by keeping track of conversations in a journal	360° survey of coworkers and friends at the end of the year
Social Health	Too many random meetings	100 meals and coffees with: 1. An encouragement 2. A learning	Keep list on spreadsheet and keep visible
Spiritual Health	Want to be more consistent in reading the Bible	Leverage a Bible reading plan for consistency	Check in with Wednesday morning guys

You may not be in charge, but you are in charge of you!

Remember, this will not happen on its own. *You may not be in charge, but you are in charge of you!* If you do not formulate a "Lead Me Plan," no one will make it for you. The responsibility is yours. But if you do, the good news is that you will be one step closer to becoming a better leader.

TIME TO LEAVE

I mentioned earlier that there might be times when you need to consider leaving a job because of an unhealthy relationship with your boss. This is, admittedly, a complicated challenge, and I won't be able to cover every situation. But the truth is that if you find yourself in the challenging position of working for someone you feel cannot lead you, you might need to leave. But before you decide to leave, I'd suggest working through a few things, just to make sure you are leaving for the right reasons. It's similar to the "Here's what we need to do before we leave our house for vacation" list my wife and I have. "Did we turn the AC off, flush the toilets, take the trash out, and lock the doors?" This list is intended to help you think through the things you need to do before you leave a messy situation.

Drop the expectations.

Hopefully, you can push past the temptation to throw all the expectations of leadership on your boss. If you feel frustrated because someone hasn't led you well, often just dropping the expectations can really change things. One of the most freeing steps for you and for your boss would be for you to relieve your boss of the obligation of leading you well.

I've worked for bosses that I've loved and I've worked for bosses that were less than loveable. Expectations always affect relationships. They just do. Obviously, unmet expectations have a way of ruining relationships because trust is broken. If you have a boss who is not meeting your expectations, I think it's fair to assess your own expectations of that person. Have you attached unreasonable expectations to the relationship? Are you asking for something that just isn't going to happen? Are you expecting to be led by someone who is incapable of providing that kind of leadership?

Of course, it's fair to have expectations of a boss. You should expect to be treated with dignity and respect. You should expect to be compensated fairly for your work. However, choosing to drop the expectations that might be unreasonable might just be what your relationship needs. Choosing to believe that your boss owes you nothing might just change everything.

Go ahead and try to say it out loud: "My boss owes me nothing." I can't promise that'll feel good, but I do believe it's worth a shot. Choosing to believe your boss owes you nothing, or at least very little, is a powerful step forward for the relationship.

Go all-in.

If you're not all-in, go all-in. Commit to the job for a significant season. Sometimes, when you feel you're not being led well, it might be because your boss doesn't feel that you're committed. It's amazing how we as humans have the innate ability to perceive someone's commitment to us. To protect ourselves, we resist going all-in with someone who is not all-in with us. If you're not committed to your boss, your boss probably won't be committed to you.

So, how do you know if you're all-in? Let me ask you a tough question: if you were to leave, would anyone be surprised? If no one would be surprised, you haven't committed enough. If you do decide to leave, the people that work around you should be surprised that you're leaving because you were all-in.

Commitment in relationships goes both ways. Sure, we all wish our bosses would lead and show their commitment to us, but it doesn't always work that way. Your boss might not be the healthiest person. People that were in your role before you may have burned your boss. If you knew more of the story, you might understand why your boss doesn't seem committed to you. Go ahead and put the ring on the finger. See if it changes the relationship. I think Beyoncé is right: the ring takes the relationship to the next level. Don't wait on your boss. Go ahead and put it on 'em.

Learn what you need to learn.

To think God cannot use bad leaders to grow a church, organization, or even you is ludicrous. God has used bad leaders for generations. Where would we be if Daniel had said, "I just can't learn under Nebuchadnezzar. I need to leave." The *church* at large wouldn't be what it is today if it always took great leaders to get stuff done! I say that because too many young leaders seem shocked to have had bad bosses. Sometimes, if our boss isn't the greatest of bosses, we act like God is not in the situation. I imagine God just shaking his head, thinking, *If you only knew how many bad bosses I've used over the years.*

What if God wants to accomplish something in you more than he wants to accomplish something through you? What if the only way for him to grow it in you is to put you under a bad leader? Don't we all learn more from times of struggle than we do from times of ease? Of course we do. When I desire what God wants to teach me more than I desire getting done what I want to get done, I am in the best place. It would be tragic for you to leave before you have learned what God wants you to learn!

Checking the boxes before you decide to leave is about leaving well. It's about learning what you need to learn before you leave. But, of course, after all the boxes have been checked, it still might be time to leave. You may have done everything you can do to make the best out of the situation you're in, and the only solution is to leave. At some point, many of us are going to be in situations where leaving is the most courageous move possible. If that's the spot you're in, I'm praying for you now. Working for a bad boss is tough enough. And leaving a job is not an easy thing to do. Knowing when and if to leave is sometimes tricky. It's rarely crystal clear, but if more than a few of these signs are present, it might be as clear as it will get.

- If you dread going to work and are miserable every day . . .
- If your lack of passion has rendered you ineffective . . .
- If the requirements of the position are hurting you or your family . . .
- If you're experiencing emotional stress due to your boss . . .
- If you aren't receiving proper compensation . . .
- If your responsibilities continue to increase but the pay doesn't . . .
- If you're unable to trust your boss because of unethical behavior . . .
- If those around you agree that a new opportunity is too good to pass up . . .
- If God has clearly called you to leave . . .

You were created with inalienable rights as a human being and as a child of God, but you were also created with inalienable responsibilities as a leader. Do not miss what God has for you by failing to lead yourself well. Perhaps God has put you in the position you are in to help you learn what you need to learn to lead yourself well. If you lead yourself well, you will ensure that you are always led well, whether you are under a great boss or not!

CHAPTER 5

CHOOSE
POSITIVITY

Learning to lead when you're not in charge is not a linear process. Your identity is always evolving. Becoming a leader doesn't follow an undergraduate course catalogue. There is no 101, 201, or 301 course flow that takes you through developing the depth of character, confidence, and composure required for good leadership. It's more of an ongoing process, running parallel to your professional development. You never graduate from the responsibility of leading yourself, of course. That's a lifelong discipline. And the good news is that you're never too young to begin and you're never too old to pick it back up. Just because we're moving on to the next chapter, don't turn the figurative page on allowing God to develop a deep-rooted sense of identity based on what he says about you. And please do not turn the page on the challenge to lead yourself. Those two foundational pursuits provide the tracks for the locomotive of leadership.

When I experienced that moment of clarity in Andy's office a few years ago, I resolved to become the leader I wanted to be, the leader I knew I could be, and the leader God calls me to be. To do that, there were some practical behaviors that needed my attention and intention. The next few chapters unpack those behaviors, and they will help you develop into the kind of leader who can effectively lead others, even when you're not in charge.

PERSPECTIVE IS EVERYTHING

I have a certain way in which I see the world. You have it too. Every human on planet earth does. It's what makes us unique. When I was in fourth grade, I remember getting a sticker of a thumb that read, "I'm Thumb-body." It's true. And so are you. And what makes me the "thumb-body" I am is how I "thee the world." I'll th-top with that for now.

One of the greatest differences in the way each of us sees the world is in how we define the word *"vacation."* My wife, Jenny, and I couldn't be more different on this.

- I want to see new places. She wants to lie on a beach and read a new book.
- I want to get to the airport just before they shut the gate. She wants to arrive two hours early. She wants enough time for them to actually change our gate to a different gate. I would like to be goosed by the Jetway door as it closes. "Oh, hello! Just in time!"
- I want to put on headphones and listen to music on the plane. She wants deep, intimate conversation, just barely loud enough to be heard over the hum of the plane. On our honeymoon, just after I put my headphones on, she pulled them out with a confused look. "I thought we were going to talk." Oh, but of course! Let's talk.
- I want to eat myself sick all week. I would like the last morsel of cheesecake to fall into my mouth just before I fall asleep. She wants to work out every day.

- I can't sleep past 7:00 a.m., even on vacation. Jenny doesn't want to even think about getting out of bed before 9:00 a.m.

You're welcome to circle the ways you see vacation, just to prove how right I am. Then send me a screenshot so I can share that with my wife and show her how right I am. Despite what she says, the way I think about a vacation is obviously the right way to see it, because it's the way I see vacation happening. I'm only half kidding about this.

In *Seven Habits of Highly Successful People*, Steven Covey says, "We see the world, not as it is, but as we are—or as we're conditioned to see it."[1] How we see the world has less to do with the way the *world is* and more to do with the way *we are*. That situation at work that's frustrating you might have more to do with you than the situation itself. And to understand how to effectively work and lead under someone else's leadership, you have to understand this matter of perspective.

I think Covey's next comment is also worth noting. "We must look *at* the lens through which we see the world, as well as the world we see and that the lens itself shapes how we interpret the world."[2] When we're trying to understand our role and how to find satisfaction in our job even when we lack the power of authority to effect change, we must first look at the lens through which we see the world.

I deeply believe this is true. How do I know?

Because somewhere in this grand world, there is someone who has a similar skill set, educational background, and amount of experience as you, is in a similar job, at a similar church or organization, has similar challenges—and actually likes the situation, because of the way he or she sees it.

There is someone, somewhere facing a similar situation and is seeing life with a lens that allows them to have more influence, excitement, and contentment. You can either let that frustrate you or you can learn from this. Personally, I'll choose to learn from it.

How you see your world shapes your world. And you have a say in how you see.

THE PANORAMIC OPTION

In 2013, Apple released the iPhone 4 and like addicts, we lined up for blocks to get our paws on the newest piece of technology from Jobs and Wozniak. With the iPhone 4, there was a new panoramic option on the camera that was creating lots of buzz. The new feature allowed horizontal, elongated pictures with a 180-degree field of view. In the past, this unique perspective was only possible by taking multiple pictures and "Photoshopping" them together or by taking out a second mortgage to purchase an extra-wide-angle, fish-eye lens to capture the shot.

The brilliance of the panoramic option was that it gave iPhone owners the possibility of capturing 180-degree beauties right from the phone in their pocket. The process of making something beautiful was made efficient. If a picture is worth a thousand words, a panoramic photo is novel-esque. There is something powerful about being able to see, in a two-dimensional photograph, something akin to what our eyes behold in reality. The panoramic picture captures a realistic viewpoint and allows you to study it to appreciate dimensions of beauty you may not have noticed before.

I have a similar experience when I travel and see different

parts of the world. My eyes are open to the world around me every day, of course, but when I get away to a new environment, I see things from a different vantage point. I may be looking at something familiar, but because of where I am, I'm looking at it differently. The more I see of the world, the *better* I see my own world. And the better you see your world, the more informed and equipped you will be to make wise decisions. Understanding can help you develop patience, graciousness, and greater discernment for all of life. A wider angle brings a wiser perspective.

I call this the ability to see the world with a panoptic lens. It's the ability to see how things fit together. It's about seeing how you fit into God's big picture. It's seeing your organization's big picture and how you can contribute. You'll need to fight to see things from this perspective, and you must constantly work to broaden your view. As you seek this wide-lens perspective, you may be able to better see and feel how your role is connected to what the organization is ultimately trying to do.

Your church or organization has a mission. And your church or organization probably has a unique vision. Even if your boss (or bosses) hasn't made them clear, they're there. You don't have to wait until someone makes them clear for you to make them clear for yourself. While it may be your manager's responsibility to communicate the mission and vision, responsibility for learning them is yours. And once you've found that "why we exist" piece, smack-dab at the top of your job responsibilities should be connecting your specific role to that overall mission and vision. This isn't a onetime thing. It's part of your everyday duties as you serve the organization and follow whomever God has placed in leadership over you.

SATISFACTION, VALUE, AND MEANING

Researchers have identified this panoptic view as one of the key drivers for employee satisfaction. They've found that the satisfaction employees have in their job is directly correlated to their ability to see how what they do fits into the big picture. Once you embrace the panoptic view, you will

The satisfaction employees have in a job is directly correlated to their ability to see how what they do fits into the big picture.

begin to make better sense of all things—the smallest of details and the largest of challenges.

Feeling valued and finding meaning as an employee goes far beyond compensation and appreciation. Dale Carnegie Training developed a white paper a few years ago titled "What Drives Employee Engagement and Why It Matters." Their research describes the evolution required for employees to move from feeling "esteemed" to "involved" to "enthusiastic" to eventually becoming a "Builder Employee."[3] This is the person willing to go the extra mile in customer service, spreads enthusiasm across their team, and take the success of the church or organization personally. So, what does it take for employees to move from mildly engaged to deeply engaged? Those leaders who feel a strong sense of ownership and have made the crucial connection between what their job is and how it drives results for the organization are more deeply engaged.[4]

Notice the key points of that conclusion. Leaders who feel

a strong sense of ownership are leaders who connect their job to the results of the organization. That's the essence of seeing your job through the panoptic lens. And you can make the choice today to begin to see the big picture.

What you're doing matters most in light of what your organization is trying to accomplish. Of course, your boss carries responsibility for helping you make that connection, but it's also your responsibility. It's your responsibility to look for ways to connect what you do each day to those overall goals and objectives. You've probably heard the phrase, "You can lead a horse to water, but you can't make it drink." Your manager can make the connection clear or he or she can make it muddy, but it's your duty to hold that objective in front of you.

I've had bosses who naturally did this well and others who didn't. In both cases, I've had to keep my eye on the big picture, and that has helped me develop a sense of commitment, even when I've had what felt like a minuscule role. It's also important to remember that there's always more going on than what I can see. God is always working on something in me and I can rarely see it while it's happening. There is no wasted time in God's economy. When you keep your focus on that, it helps you keep the perspective you need to be able to dig in deeply where God has put you.

THE PANOPTIC PYRAMID

Seeing with a panoptic view is a posture for leadership. It's built on a deep trust in God and a persistent hope in the future. When you work to see the big picture, it will also help you get behind your leader, even if they aren't the best. You'll wear the team jersey, even when you might disagree. You'll start to feel owner-ship, even for decisions you didn't make. To help me connect the way I view things with the results I experience in my life and in my job, I've developed this crazy-looking pyramid:

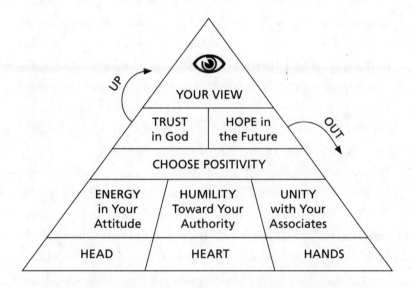

Here's how to try out this posture for yourself. You already have a lens through which you're seeing your current situation. Maybe it's the way you see your relationship with your boss. Maybe it's the way you see your work, feeling it doesn't make a difference. All leaders have something or someone informing how they see their situation. Consider the apostle Paul. I find it fascinating to read his letter to the Philippians while thinking about where he was when he wrote it. Four times in the first chapter, Paul explicitly refers to the chains he is wearing as he writes.

Now I've never spent a night in jail, but I did get sent to detention a few times in high school. I remember the mood I was in. I wasn't fit to write anything positive about the world. My view on the world was fearful, angry, and quite negative. Not Paul, though. Paul was *in chains* when he wrote the following verses: "Now I want you to know, brothers and sisters, that what has happened to me has actually served to *advance the gospel*. As a result, it has become clear throughout the whole palace guard and to everyone else that I am in chains for Christ" (Phil. 1:12–13, emphasis mine).

What the what? Somehow, some way, Paul was able to lift his head in the midst of his dark situation and see the bigger picture of the opportunities in front of him. He was convinced God was up to something, despite his situation. His chains said that he was useless, facing a dead end. But he did not allow the chains to determine his vision. Instead, he saw his chains through a panoptic view. Instead of limiting his ministry, the chains now appeared useful, indicating he was blessed and advancing God's purposes.

The way you see is more important than the tragedy.

The way you see is stronger than any calamity.

The way you see is bigger than the details of the catastrophe.

I know your job right now is not a tragedy or a calamity or a catastrophe, but when the wave of rhymes is rolling, I've learned to get on the surfboard and ride. I am saying that if you are frustrated with your job because you don't have the seniority you feel you need, you don't have the authority you were told you'd have, or you don't have control over the decision-making to be able to effect the change you want to make, don't give up! Don't settle! Don't let the frustration you feel over what you don't have keep you from doing what you can do. Changing your perspective on your situation can change everything. Seeing what you *do* have will allow you to overcome what you don't.

Paul got this. Somehow he didn't get lost in the weeds and miss what was in front of him. Paul's panoptic vision told him, "I'm not chained to this prison guard. This prison guard is chained to me!" He stayed true to his calling even when the odds were stacked against him. He kept his eyes up even when his feet were in chains. I want what he had. If Paul had this view in prison, hopefully, it's possible for you and me to have it where God has put us.

WHAT INFORMS YOUR VIEW?

What you believe about God and how you see the future are foundational voices for how you will lead right now. A small view of God leads to an outlook of despair. An outlook of despair for the future will lead to being consumed with your present circumstances. Looking again at Paul's letter to the Philippians, we see this was true for him. The two pillars that supported Paul's panoptic view were his trust in God and his hope for the future. These two foundations allowed Paul to see what the normal person couldn't. No matter what was happening or what was going to happen, Paul's perspective allowed him to bow his knee to his boss (his jailer) while maintaining a strong drive and passion for what God was going to do in the future. It allowed him to stand firm when the footing of his circumstances was wobbly. Listen to how Paul sees God at work in his circumstances: "I will continue to rejoice, for I know that through your prayers and God's provision of the Spirit of Jesus Christ *what has happened to me will turn out for my deliverance*" (Phil. 1:18–19, emphasis mine).

Paul is in chains, imprisoned without good reason. Yet he maintains a deep belief that God is going to deliver him one way or another. Paul's remarkable trust in God's provision informed his view. And that means when the circumstances of your job feel shaky, trusting in God will help to stabilize you as well. There is a confidence that comes from believing that God has you where he wants you. Throughout history, God has put specific people into particular positions for definitive reasons. And he has you where he wants you.

But notice that it wasn't just a deep trust in God that affected Paul's outlook. Being convinced that God was up to something greater than the circumstances in front of him provided a spirit of expectancy and hopefulness that allowed Paul to maintain a sense of positivity. He said, "I eagerly *expect* and *hope* that I will in no way be ashamed, but will have sufficient courage so that now as always *Christ will be exalted* in my body, whether by life or by death" (Phil. 1:20, emphasis mine).

Hope is a confident expectation of something good to come. The basis of our Christian faith is that our God is a God who is always able, always moving, and always working on our behalf. Even when it feels like he's silent, he's never distant. Even when it feels like it's over, hope allows us to trust because of what we believe about our God. The resurrection of Jesus is the most poignant, powerful, and perfect picture of hope I can imagine. If forgiveness and death are the two greatest enemies we face, the resurrection provides victory over both. As followers of Jesus, we should be the most hope-filled people on the planet.

Paul was ever hope-filled. The resurrection provided him with the basis for his calling and purpose on earth. Any suffering he faced was worthwhile in his mind because of the hope he had that God could use it. Hope moved Paul to choose a positive outlook in suffering and in success, in poverty and in riches, in sickness and in health.

Trust in God and hope for the future are the legs you and I stand on. If we have a God who is able to provide in life or in death and a God who is able to restore, heal, and use circumstances in this life and the next, what could we ever face that would undo what he's done? Those two truths are heavy enough to be counterweights to lift our perspective on anything.

WHAT DOES YOUR VIEW PRODUCE?

When these powerful truths become the foundation for how you see, you can do the inconceivable. You can choose positivity. This is not just positive thinking, a self-delusion that ignores reality. It's based on a different perspective of your reality, a panoptic view of your circumstances. Trust-fueled, hope-filled, forward-thinking people can push through anything that gets in the way because their eyes are fixed on more than what's directly in front of them.

And it is a choice—one you can make today! This positivity is not just a personality trait. Positivity is a *character* trait. Personality refers to our inherent bent, much of which is predetermined. But character is developed over time. And more often than not, character is developed when things are difficult. The lunchroom doesn't develop muscle; the weight room develops muscle. And you'll find that the hardest time to choose positivity is when you're handed a decision you didn't make and might not like.

You have to teach the outline you didn't create.

You have to manage the volunteer process you didn't come up with.

You have to make the announcement about the event you would've never attended.

In Patrick Lencioni's book *The Advantage*,[5] he argues that people are more likely to buy in when they've had the opportunity to weigh in. But that doesn't always happen, does it? When the team is small enough for you to weigh in on all the decisions, it's easy to buy into the decision that's made. But it's challenging to choose positivity when you are asked to buy into an opportunity you didn't weigh in on. No one asked your opinion; they just made a decision. Worse, you weren't even invited to the meeting! I used to think that the higher up I moved in the organization, the less my feelings would be hurt when I wasn't invited to a meeting. Wrong! The higher up I move, the more my feelings are hurt when I'm not invited to a meeting. And it's even worse when they make a decision in the meeting and then ask me to execute it. Seriously? And on top of that, I find myself thinking the decision they've made is terrible!

When I'm not part of the decision-making process, my default response is to check out, to abdicate my opportunity to lead. When I'm handed a decision I think is dumb or wrong or less-than-best, my default is to sit back and throw my hands up. I think, *Since this is clearly not going to work, I'll just sit back and let them see how bad this idea really is. If they wanted this to work, they would've invited me to the meeting, and I would've given them an idea that would have been great. Instead, I'll just sit back and watch this train wreck happen*. That kind of rotten attitude doesn't win in leadership. It won't make you a better leader either. It's the easy way out. Instead, you can choose positivity—even when you didn't have a say in the decision. More important than making the right decision is owning the decision handed to you and making it right. Positivity will help you with this.

Why do positive people make good leaders? Because positivity is attractive and produces other qualities in leaders that are naturally attractive to others. Leaders who exude positivity will begin to see their influence grow. Below are some of the by-products of a broader perspective.

Energy in Your Attitude

I'm not sure there is anything directly under my control that can have a more powerful impact on others than the attitude I choose. The greatest benefit I bring my team is not my talents, gifts, experience, or education. It's my energy.

Leaders who bring a trust-fueled, hope-filled, forward-thinking attitude every day can change any team dynamic. And you don't have to be the senior pastor or a CEO. You can pack this attitude in your lunch box tomorrow, and it has the potential to change the climate of your workplace. You might be an invisible intern with no authority or a mid-level manager who feels stuck, but if you choose to bring the attitude of a 100-watt bulb, you'll start seeing things light up. You can't just try this once, though. And that's where it becomes a discipline you cultivate. This needs to be the attitude you choose daily, like a mail carrier. Come rain, hail, sleet, snow, or sun, you determine that you will have an attitude of positivity, regardless of the circumstances.

Humility Toward Those in Authority

You are not ready for your boss's job. Why would I say that? Because you're not in your boss's job. If you unpack what Paul says in Romans 13:1, he, by the inspiration of the Holy Spirit, makes it pretty clear: "Let everyone be subject to the governing authorities, for there is no authority except that which God has established. *The authorities that exist have been established by God*" (emphasis mine). This is a pretty weighty thing to think about. It's God, not man, who ultimately establishes authority. If someone is in charge, God has a reason. Now before you offer me thirty objections to this, I will admit that none of us can fully understand how that works. Do we have free will? Yes. The Bible is clear that we make our own choices and we're held responsible for them. But we are also told that if someone is in a position of authority, God had something to do with it. At the very least, this passage means God has established the system of how humans work through authority, and working against that system means working against God.

Let me be clear, though, because this passage would seem to imply and even encourage a passive acceptance of the status quo. I don't think that's what Paul had in mind. We know this because of the context in which he is writing. This was a tense time for Paul. He was working tirelessly for progress. Knowing that God is the ultimate authority isn't something Paul tells the church in order to encourage passivity. He shares this truth to encourage them to have a risk-taking faith that follows God, stands for the truth, and pursues God's kingdom agenda. But Paul doesn't want Christians to think that authority is a bad thing in and of itself. God has a purpose for the structures of power that exist in this world, and though they will not last forever, we can trust God is at work through them and in them. Even in your organization. Even through that boss you don't like very much. This should also encourage us to pray. Because if you don't have the authority you would like to have, one of the best ways to change that is to take it up with God.

What Romans 13:1 tells me is that if I'm frustrated with the job I don't have, maybe I still have work to do. If you think you should be promoted and you haven't been promoted yet, perhaps there's still some growth God has planned for you. When you're ready and when the time is right, God may lift you up. Or he may take you down a different path. You can get mad, or you can get busy getting better. You get to choose. A deep trust in God and a persistent hope for the future will push you to keep growing and learning because you believe God is getting you ready for something he will lift you into. Until he does, you're not quite ready. This kind of humility allows me to keep working on my craft, knowing that when I'm ready, my time will come.

Unity with Your Associates

Do you remember those birds in *Finding Nemo*? They get me every time. As they fight for what's on the ground, they are flying around screaming, "Mine! Mine! Mine!" Never has Disney nailed a picture of the selfish human condition better than in that little scene. Sadly, we do the same thing. Our tendency is to fly around screaming, "Mine! Mine! Mine!" We do that with our ideas, our projects, our ministries, and our roles. Choosing positivity forces us to recognize that whatever we have has been given to us as gifts to develop. That tends to work against our selfish pride. You'll find you are more willing to take *your* ideas, lay them down, and partner up with others so that you can all get behind the same plan.

The panoptic view fights for *we* over *me*. The panoptic view tells us that we're better together than we are apart. Choosing positivity produces collective results greater than if we were each pushing our own agenda.

THE FINAL LIFT

My favorite condescending question on planet earth is, "Do you even lift, bro?" Anytime a friend of mine tries to challenge me about anything, that's my go-to response. This sarcastic little question probably started in weightlifting circles as a way to aggravate that guy posing as a fitness expert. And if you'll allow me, I think there's a spiritual axiom for us wrapped up in this silly question.

Who does the *lifting* for your career? Think about where you are today. How did you get there? In every story, there are people involved who were instrumental in lifting us up, giving us a leg up. Parents, teachers, coaches, friends—we all have people who have been key in our advancement. Obviously, we must do a great deal of that lifting ourselves. You absolutely have something to do with where you are today, but you and I know that, ultimately, we aren't the ones doing the heavy lifting. There is someone else behind every story—the one who actually has the most influence on the situation. The one who is the hero behind the star. Our Creator and heavenly Father plays that role. He's the one who puts people on stages, turns the spotlight on, and gives them the microphone. He's the one who hands the gavel to the judge, the whistle to the coach, and the touchscreen plasma to the teacher.

"Humble yourselves, therefore, under God's mighty hand, that he may lift you up in due time" (1 Peter 5:6). This little verse is so simple and it assigns two roles quite clearly. So let me ask you again. "Do you even lift, bro?" When it comes down to it, you don't. God does the lifting. We need to do the humbling. God picks people up. We need to keep our heads down and work hard. Followers of Christ know that we are who we are and are where we are today because of God. Because God's mighty hand is strong enough to lift any of us up out of any circumstance, we can trust him and we can have hope for the future.

No one knows "due time" like God does. Too many of us think "due time" means "right after we pray."

"God, it's Monday. I've been in this job for six whole months now and I haven't been promoted. If I don't hear something from my boss by Friday, I'm going to start looking for another job. I'm due for that promotion!"

Keep in mind that you and I are the same people who burn our mouths on Hot Pockets. Maybe we're not the best judges of our "due times."

A few years ago, I watched a documentary called *Muscle Shoals*.[6] This northern Alabama town, with a population of around 13,000, is plagued with poverty and racial hostility. But in this forgotten town, a guy named Rick Hall founded FAME (Florence Alabama Music Enterprises), which has produced some of the most influential music of the last fifty years. Take a look at the artists that have recorded in Muscle Shoals: Etta James, Otis Redding, Percy Sledge, Wilson Pickett, and Donny Osmond. And that's just the short list.

Since I grew up in Alabama, I had heard of Muscle Shoals. I had driven through this small town located on the banks of the Tennessee River a time or two, but I had no clue as to the level of musical genius that had recorded there. Because of the egalitarian and racially inclusive culture created at FAME, this tiny town—hardly even on the map—has become one of the top recording destinations in the world. Watching the documentary, I realized: *If you are creating something great, your time will come.* And if your time hasn't come yet, keep working to create something great.

I've had many days where I've thought, *I don't think my bosses see what I can really do.* But instead of allowing that thought to take me down the path of pride and bitterness, I've tried to stay low, humble, and hungry. If your bosses haven't noticed your contributions yet, you're welcome to get mad and frustrated. You're welcome to point your finger and blame the one you think is keeping something from you. But I don't think that will help you grow as a leader. It might feel good for a moment, but over the long haul, it may actually work against you. I think a better option is to trust God and have patience. Focus on cultivating the panoptic view and waiting for the opportunities God will provide. You can take all the energy you're using to be mad or frustrated and use it to improve. Channel that energy toward hard work. Maybe, if your skills have not been noticed, it's because your skills have not been developed like they need to be.

As you begin to see your job, your calling, and your life as God wants you to see them, with the big picture in mind, it will help lessen the frustration that can destroy you—and the team you work on. And as you begin to see your life with the big picture in mind, you'll be better able to choose the positivity God wants you to have.

CHAPTER 6

THINK
CRITICALLY

Maybe you are one of those people who, after finishing the previous chapter, feels a little sick at the idea of being positive all the time. You are wired to be a realist. And you know that positivity alone—all the time—will drive you and the people you work with crazy. I have good news for you. I agree. That's why positivity doesn't stand alone. We need to couple it with the skill of thinking critically. Learning how to exercise the skill of thinking critically for the good of others is essential to leading when you're not in charge.

THE RAINBOW-PUKING UNICORN

Fill in the blank on this one. There are two kinds of personalities in the world: positive and _____.

If you put the word "negative" in the blank, you're not entirely wrong. You're just mislabeling people. I've come to believe there aren't "negative" people in the world. What I mean is that most people won't willingly self-identify as "negative." When you ask these people what they are, they will tell you they are just "realistic." I love that word.

It's an interesting fact of life that I can't prove but believe is true—positive personalities typically marry realists. For some reason, that positive person is just naturally attracted to that realist . . . and vice versa. Maybe they each recognize they need the other to survive the challenges of raising children. I know Jenny and I are well suited for each other in this way. I'm just naturally a positive person. It's a strength *and* a weakness. It provides me resiliency and helps me push through difficult situations, but it can also make me fairly naive to challenges ahead. I'm guilty at over promising and under delivering. "Oh, hey babe. Yeah, I'm almost done. I should be home in twenty minutes." Jenny has learned that's code for "I'll see you in an hour."

Over the past few years, I've been creating a list of criteria for the consummate leader who leverages influence and not authority to get stuff done. I've noticed that choosing the panoptic view is massively important. Leaders need to cultivate a positive vision in those they lead. And they need to see that vision for themselves. But a positive perspective alone can be dangerous if it's not coupled with what we talk about in this chapter.

Most people are slightly nauseated by overly positive people. I know that's how I feel, even though I'm a generally positive person. I'm immediately skeptical about people who constantly speak to me in emphatic and optimistic terms.

"Sunday was the best ever!"

"That sermon was the greatest sermon I've ever heard in this church."

"I've never had a more powerful worship moment."

Really? The best ever? In your entire life, this is the most powerful experience of worship you've ever had? Maybe that's true, but when someone says that every other week, I tend to not take them seriously. Despite what the minifigures in *The LEGO Movie* try to sell us, everything is not always awesome. If you believe you're stuck in denial, I'd suggest you marry a realist.

A few years ago, we launched a service at our church that was designed for twenty-somethings. It has been a huge wind of momentum for us. We were trying to make sure that any twenty-four-year-old professional living in our community had a place to belong and a place where he or she could invite an unchurched friend. We started doing all the research we could on what the future of the church would look like by talking to everyone we knew under the age of thirty. Because I was spending so much time on this, people inside and outside our organization started forwarding me any article with the word "millennial" in the title. As a side note, if I were a millennial, and I'm barely not a millennial, I would be very sick of people writing articles about me. Let's just say my inbox was flooded.

There was one article that just knocked me over because the title was so funny and eye-catching. To the best of my memory, it read: "Millennials: Are they a group of misguided optimists or a group of rainbow-puking unicorns?"

Rainbow-puking unicorns. That is hands down *the* greatest image my mind has literally ever conceived. Ever. (Sorry for the ridiculous positivity, but in this case, it's actually true.) Doesn't that do such a fantastic job of describing some of those positive people you know? Hear me out. Positivity is great, but a rainbow-puking unicorn is not. It's sick, and not in the good way. That's why in this chapter I want to introduce you to a skill that will keep you from being one of those obnoxious, nauseating, overly positive, planted-in-denial, rainbow-puking unicorn people. When this skill is coupled with a genuinely positive, hope-filled perspective, you can become an effective and balanced leader with the ability to add lift to any room and add value to whatever team God places you.

CRITICAL THINKING AS A SKILL

One of the most common frustrations of not being in charge is being told no. No one likes being told no. But even worse than being told no is being given a task to work on and receiving little to no direction. Then, after you spend energy, effort, and time on said project, you are told, "That's not exactly what we're looking for. What else you got?"

A few years ago, our campus leadership had an idea about how to engage new guests through a new, concierge-type environment. Our team discussed the idea, created a plan, and even implemented a trial run to see how it would look in real life. Someone from our central team heard about it, and we were given orders to cease and desist because it felt different than the way we were doing it at our other campuses. I didn't like that. So I dug in through a few challenging conversations. I began to understand why they wanted us to wait, but that didn't stop me from feeling frustrated. I thought that if I were in charge, I could just say, "Go do it!" and it would be done. Instead, I had to wait to implement a great idea because someone higher up didn't think it was the best idea for us.

In these moments, we are most susceptible to believing the lie that we must be in charge in order to get done what we want to get done. And rather than becoming uber positive and blindly supporting everything that's handed to us, or becoming cynical, bitter, and negative, we need to respond critically and thought-fully. Choose positivity, but also think critically.

THE NUTS AND BOLTS OF CRITICAL THINKING

Every good leader is also a critical thinker. Leaders intuitively know how to make something better. At the conferences our church hosts for young leaders, my boss, Andy Stanley, always tells the crowd that we know they probably have two sets of notes: one for what they are learning and another for what they would do differently if this were their conference. That's what critical-thinking leaders do. And you can hardly turn it off. You will always be looking for ways to make things better, to say things better, to do things better. That's what leaders do.

> Every good leader is also a critical thinker.

But leaders who are critical thinkers don't just criticize and whine; they learn. They start by questioning things. Why do we do it this way? Is there a better way? What would happen if we stopped that? Why is this working? What's the real "win" here? Asking questions is at the heart of critical thinking. Questions challenge assumptions. Questions uncover the invisible forces behind behaviors and actions.

Critical thinkers also notice things. Why is there no music playing? Why were their greeters so old? That presentation lacked empathy. I wonder why they chose not to paint that sign the same color as the rest of their signs. Being observant is another key leadership quality, because as we carefully observe things, we are able to better determine cause-and-effect relationships.

Leaders know what to pay attention to and can find the variable that has changed or is out of place and is causing a certain result.

Critical thinkers are also able to *connect* things. Similar to the ability to observe, critical thinkers are able to observe and then make connections between seemingly disconnected behaviors and feelings. They also have the ability to identify what they feel in certain environments. And even more important, critical thinkers can identify what's causing that feeling. They are self-aware and have the innate skill of connecting the feelings people have to the contributing behaviors causing those feelings. The brilliance of this kind of leadership is that when you learn to anticipate those feelings before they happen, you can align the team to create an environment that will elicit the feelings you desire for them.

Great leaders who lead great organizations do this week in and week out. At the helm, you'll find leaders who ask questions and connect their observations in ways that others just can't. Then they find simple ways to communicate these connections to volunteers who feel valued and part of the process. They implement this week after week to the benefit of the community. Everything is not always awesome. Great leaders know that. But they also know how to listen, watch, connect the dots, and fix problems because they're able to think critically.

THE TOUGHER ROAD

Colin Cowherd, one of the leading American sports media personalities, is known for his strong opinions. I find him not only entertaining, but also insightful. For instance, in *You Herd Me*, he says, "Social Media: Don't do it after a cocktail or in your underwear."[1] Think about how much nonsense would be avoided if we applied that rule. Cowherd himself is a critical thinker and what he says about NFL quarterbacks caught my attention. He began to notice that the NFL was filled with quarterbacks from small colleges. The traditional powerhouses in college football (Alabama, LSU, Florida, Clemson, Florida State, Southern Cal, Notre Dame, Michigan, Ohio State, Oklahoma, Texas) have only produced a few of the current starting NFL quarterbacks. Why is that? Cowherd points to a few reasons:

- The quarterbacks from small colleges tend to have a chip on their shoulder because they've been overlooked. A professor told Aaron Rodgers that he would never make it.[2] Matt Ryan was passed over by all the big colleges.
- Small colleges allow these quarterbacks to develop skills they wouldn't otherwise develop at larger schools. Ben Roethlisberger learned how to maneuver in broken pockets because of the lightly recruited offensive linemen at Miami University. (Not the 'U' of Miami, Florida, but Miami of Ohio, which is known more for their high percentage of co-eds than their athletic department.)

These players have a high "with it" factor. They're sharp. They're present. They're smart. They connect the dots. They understand how to motivate people. And I think an unstated reason these quarterbacks from small, lesser-known football schools succeed is because they learn critical thinking in these environments. They face a tougher road to the NFL, and that road prepares them to be better leaders at the next level. Remember, leadership is the ability to motivate people to work harder, longer, and smarter, because the vision of the end goal has been painted so clearly. Those who must overcome obstacles need to push themselves to think critically, and that helps them when they reach the next level.

FOUR SUBTLE SHIFTS

While positivity is largely a choice we make to embrace a panoptic view or perspective, being a critical thinker isn't a choice; it's a skill. It's a skill that can be developed. If you're not great at critical thinking, you can grow in this area and become a better critical thinker.

Since I've been a bit negative on positivity this chapter, it bears repeating: the greatest benefit you bring your team is your positive energy. But being a critical thinker is a substantial value-add. It involves questioning assumptions, noticing abnormalities, and connecting the dots between feelings and actions. These skills will help you solve problems. If you're seeking to develop this skill, there are a few subtle shifts you can immediately make. I've seen these effectively produce long-term results in a leader's ability to influence others.

Shift #1: Stop thinking as an employee. Start thinking as an owner.

I've heard this so many times at leadership conferences and on leadership podcasts that I almost didn't include it. But it's just so true. Nothing has affected my ability to think critically more over the last few years than trying to think like an owner.

Owners see things others don't see.

Owners have more buy-in than others do.

Owners care more deeply because their future depends on it.

A few years ago, I hosted an event for Passion Conferences called Passion. I was honored to accept the invitation because I am profoundly grateful for Louie and Shelley Giglio. These two people are some of the boldest and bravest Jesus followers I've ever been around. When others ask, "Why?" Louie and Shelley are dreamers who ask, "Why not?" They have been spiritual parents to me, both directly and indirectly, to an entire generation of college-aged leaders over the last several decades. So when they asked, I immediately said yes!

Just before the event, I had a chance to sit down with Louie and ask him what he thought was the most important thing I could do as the host for their event. Without hesitating, Louie told me I needed to *own this event like it was my event.* "If you're talking about the next Passion album, you need to talk about it like it was *your* idea to record it. If you're talking about the hospital we're raising money for to help Syrian refugees, you need to talk about it like you've sat in on every meeting we've had." That was incredibly helpful, challenging, and freeing. And why is this true? A simple illustration we use all the time in our organization may help you see the difference. If there is trash in the hallway or in the parking lot, employees may decide to walk past it. Or worse, they call someone who works in facilities to pick up the trash. Owners pick up the trash because it's their reputation on the line.

I think this principle is even more important for church employees and pastors to grasp. I have zero experience working in a family-owned business, but I'd imagine that when you're working in a business and you are the son or daughter of the owner, you will naturally think differently than the other employees. Why? Because you know there is a good chance this business won't just be here for your job today—you might be the owner yourself someday. There is a healthy pride that comes from knowing that one day, you may very well be the primary leader responsible for stewarding the organization. And that's what we're doing as leaders in the church. As sons and daughters of God, we are working for our Dad, the owner.

In Romans 8:17, Paul makes this point clear: "Now if we are children, then we are heirs—heirs of God and co-heirs with Christ, if indeed we share in his sufferings in order that we may also share in his glory." If we are sons and daughters of God, then we are responsible for thinking like owners. And while this is especially true for those working in a church or religious non-profit, it's also true for those engaged in business or leading in other capacities. All of the work we do matters to God, and we will be held accountable for it all, not just the work we do for church programs or a Sunday service. You might not be in the role of senior pastor, but you should care about your work and calling because you're in God's family. You're not just a servant in the house of God. You are a child of the king and you are called to work for him wherever you are placed.

Shift #2: Stop stacking your meetings. Start scheduling thinking meetings.

If you're in a church, a small business, or working in a corporation, you may get sucked into a multitude of meetings. It's the natural gravitational pull of any organization. My favorite description of this comes from *The 4 Disciplines of Execution* by Chris McChesney, Sean Covey, and Jim Huling. The authors describe this gravitational pull toward busyness as "the whirlwind."[3] The whirlwind is described as the massive amount of energy needed to simply keep your operation going on a day-to-day basis. When

I think of the whirlwind, the first thing that comes to mind are the countless meetings that show up on my calendar. Sometimes numerous meetings just start to appear. After a while, you start wondering, *Do I run my calendar or does my calendar run me?*

The worst is having a stack of meetings, back to back. While this can seem efficient, it can also be an enemy of critical thinking. I will get to the end of my day and realize I've generated no new thoughts, no new ideas. I've only been reacting to circumstances and solving problems. If you find yourself constantly in that mode, you need to reclaim control of your life. You need to stop stacking meetings and start scheduling time to think critically. You'll never develop as a leader if you cannot master this.

Why do my best ideas come to me in the shower? I feel like my IQ is at least twenty points higher while lathering up than at any other time of the day. And I'm not alone in finding my light bulb moments there. Cognitive psychologist Scott Barry Kaufman says that seventy-two percent of people get creative ideas in the shower.[4] That's because thinking critically requires uninterrupted mental space. It's not just showering that creates these times of clarity. Mowing the grass, taking a walk, driving to work, or pausing long enough to look, observe, and connect the dots brings the space necessary to think clearly. If you're going from meeting to meeting, you will not have that space. You need to carve it out or your leadership will suffer.

I'm not suggesting that you shower between meetings, though I do think you would find more creativity in your ideas throughout the day if you did. And you'd be so fresh and so clean (thanks, Big Boi). I am, however, going to suggest that you schedule space to think critically, marking it down like a meeting, at points throughout the day. About five years ago, I started spacing out my meetings (those I could control) with more intentionality. My efficient nature wanted my meetings to end at the top of the hour and the next meeting to start sixty seconds later. But I knew I was worse off for doing this. Efficiency wasn't leading to effectiveness. I found there were a number of negative consequences. First, I was constantly late for meetings. Second, I wasn't fully present in any of the meetings. I was physically there, but I found myself processing the previous meeting and also thinking about the next one. Going from meeting to meeting caused the air traffic control of my brain to be fuzzy and distorted. I was preoccupied, distant, and mentally absent. Worst of all, I had no space to think clearly.

I made two changes. I began to schedule space between meetings, short spots of downtime for me to think. I also forced myself to get to work earlier. When I was in my twenties, I remember sitting with mentors who told me what time they arrived at work. It was ungodly and seemed impossible. And then, one day, something in me clicked, and I realized I would never be able to add value if I didn't add in time to think. Getting to work earlier helps me have that additional time, and scheduling time between meetings to think critically has enabled me to improve the quality of my contributions to those meetings. The greatest enemy of thinking critically is an overcrowded schedule. Again, own your calendar or your calendar will own you.

Shift #3: Stop being critical. Start thinking critically.

The most dangerous outcome of thinking critically is that subtle pull you feel to become a critical person. There are times that line between being critical and thinking critically is razor thin.

I've known some cynical, negative people who excuse their attitudes and behaviors, trying to pass them off as critical thinking. I can hear the cacophony of excuses.

"If you can't handle feedback, don't ask."

"How are we ever going to get better if we don't face the truth?"

"Sorry if you can't handle it. I'm just speaking the truth."

If thinking critically is a skill, being critical is a snare. And I'm choosing the word *snare* for a reason. I bumped into this word while preaching on Proverbs 29:25: "Fear of man will prove to be a snare, but whoever trusts in the LORD is kept safe." I love this axiom from King Solomon and I've learned to love the word *snare*. But what did Solomon mean? *The Bible Knowledge Commentary* says it well: "To fear man ensnares in the sense that one's actions are controlled or confined by the person who is dreaded."[5] You don't mean to get caught in a snare. You just didn't plan to avoid getting caught in it. I know that many young leaders do not want to be critical. They don't sit around planning to be cynics, but they still get caught in the trap.

Every time I talk about critical thinking with leaders, I ask this question: "What is the key difference between someone who is critical and someone who is a critical thinker?" After a few moments, someone shouts out my favorite answer.

Motive.

People who are critical want you to lose. They're motivated to tear something down. They do not offer constructive criticism; they deconstruct. They're bringing problems, not solutions. When I point out something wrong with you to make me feel better about me, I'm being critical.

People who are great critical thinkers want you to win.

They're motivated to make something better. Yes, they may deconstruct, but it's for the betterment of others. They don't even care about the credit. When I point out something wrong with what you're doing because I think I see a better way for you, I'm thinking critically to serve you.

Shift #4: Stop giving others a grade. Start lending them a hand.

No one likes feeling like they're being graded. No one likes the feeling of being constantly measured and monitored. I've felt graded by others, and I know that within me is a desire to grade others. It may not be intentional, but remember, no one intentionally steps into a snare. It's only by carelessly walking through life that we step into snares. So if you're not careful, your critical thinking will make others feel like you're giving them grades. When you stand in the back of the room evaluating the performance of another team, pay attention to your posture. Pay attention to your countenance. Pay attention to what you say when you see them next.

This is not about *whether* you should convey the thoughts that could better those around you. It's about *how* you pass on those thoughts. I'm convinced that you can say anything—even hard and honest truth—if you say it in love and with a caring tone. When you communicate critical thoughts to those beside you, below you, or to your boss, you need to do so with a helping hand, not a grading tone. Here are a few practical ways to do this:

- Assure the listener you are for him or her. When we know others are for us, we can better hear feedback that might otherwise feel critical.

- Always present a solution to any problem you raise. Issue recognition doesn't win friends.
- Keep your blood pressure as low as possible when communicating feedback. If you can't talk about it without getting emotional, you're not ready to talk about it.
- Deliver potential challenges in the rhythm of positive-challenge-positive. Some call it a compliment sandwich and some just call it wise.

Great leaders know how to communicate critical thoughts in a way that benefits others. Jesus knew just how to do it, and through the way he loved the woman at the well, the woman caught in adultery, and even his longtime disciple Peter, Jesus showed us the way.

THE POWER OF THE TOWEL

Just east of downtown Dallas sits Dallas Theological Seminary. I've spent a lot of time on that campus and feel a huge debt of gratitude to that institution. One of the most vivid images in my mind from there is a statue I passed hundreds of times. With fantastic clarity and deliberate emotion, the statue depicts a famous scene from the life of Jesus. It's a sculpture of Jesus in the upper room, just before the Passover festival, and he offers a striking model for leadership. After the dinner, Jesus does something that was and still is almost unthinkable for any leader, let alone the Savior of the world.

The apostle John sets the scene by telling us, "Jesus knew that the Father had put all things under his power" (John 13:3). This is an odd statement. Powerful people do not do what Jesus does next. John continues, "So he got up from the meal, took off his outer clothing, and wrapped a towel around his waist. After that, he poured water into a basin and began to wash his disciples' feet, drying them with the towel that was wrapped around him" (John 13:4–5).

When I was in school, I passed that statue so many times that it eventually blended into my surroundings. It became invisible to me. Then, one day, church history professor Dr. John Hannah eloquently brought this statue to life for me. At the beginning of the semester, he opened his class by telling us he was not there to give us a grade, but to give us a hand. He assured us that if we felt graded by the tests and papers, it was unintentional. He wanted us to know that his desire was to help us more than he wanted to grade us. I can still feel the genuineness of his words. Dr. Hannah's words were wonderful, and as I passed the statue again walking out of class, it immediately connected his words with those of Jesus. Jesus never held a clipboard, but if anyone had the right to grade others, it was the perfect, sinless Son of God. But that's not why he came. Jesus didn't come to condemn the world; he came to save it. He was far more interested in helping others than in grading them.

So think positively. And be a critical thinker as well. Be known as a value-add, a problem solver. As you pursue the skill of thinking critically, keep that image in mind—the picture of Jesus on his knee, towel in hand, washing the filthy feet of his closest followers. The Creator of stars and galaxies gave us a picture of what we need most—to be served and washed clean in our heart of hearts. Jesus did for us what we needed most and deserved least. He could've graded us, pointing out where we had failed and missed the mark, but he didn't. Instead, he introduced us to the radical concept of servant leadership by grabbing a towel and dropping the clipboard. Thinking critically is crucial to becoming a leader who leads when you're not in charge. And as you learn to think critically, never forget that the towel is the way God leads us, and it is always more powerful than the clipboard.

CHAPTER 7

REJECT
PASSIVITY

As an able-bodied, cheerful, and social college student who was deeply involved at an already large and continuously growing church, I was a prime candidate to help somebody move some furniture. To make matters worse, Matt BeVier, my closest friend at Georgia Tech and coleader of our high school ministry at church, owned a truck. Owning a truck is the kiss of death to your Saturday afternoon dreams of kicking your feet up and watching football. If Matt and I were more economically astute and entrepreneurial, we could've likely turned a profit from the dozens of friends and families who requested our services each week. Let's just say I never got rich moving furniture.

One of my clearest memories of our work was not something we moved, but something I learned from someone we moved. I remember a family that was upgrading homes and asked us to help them with the move. After a moving company had done the lion's share, we showed up to move one final piece—the dad's beloved pool table. It was getting moved to their new basement. Now, let me stop here and ask you: have you lifted a pool table recently? Of course not. Lifting a pool table is like trying to lift a sleeping rhinoceros. My favorite part of that job was the seventy-five-year-old, potty-mouthed grandfather who took on the role of foreman of the operation. I can't recall his name and can barely remember his face, but the sound of his cigarette-scarred, raspy southern voice is unforgettable. I felt like I was enacting a *Saturday Night Live* skit as grandpa stood around watching us eventually move the table, offering a running commentary on every misstep and wall-scrape.

He repeated one line over and over and over again, and it has stuck with me through the years. Every time I move something heavy, it pops into my head again. Anytime it looked like the pool table would win and crush us to death beneath its weight, the old man would yell in his raspy voice, "Don't let it beat cha! Don't let it beat cha!"

That day, I smirked every time he said it. But it keeps ringing in my mind, popping in there at the oddest moments. It's become something of a rallying cry for me to cultivate intentionality and assertiveness. Even though the pool table was an inanimate and mindless object, if I wasn't on top of my game, it could have and would have beaten me down.

"Don't let it beat cha!"

THE LOSS OF CONTROL

One of the benefits of being in charge, of having authority over others, is the semblance of control that authority brings. We all know that the feeling of being in control can be powerful. When I start making decisions, I experience that sense of control and I'm more naturally assertive and intentional. When I'm the one calling the shots, I enter the zone and focus. I'm personally connected to these decisions, and when I'm the one who is ultimately responsible and accountable for the outcome, I just feel more buy-in. That's why the feeling of ownership we talked about last chapter is so powerful. Owners feel a sense of control over the plan, the strategy, and the way forward for the organization. And while we all want to be in control, we shouldn't assume that this control makes it any easier, because it's not. But the feeling of control does naturally bring us more intentionality and assertiveness in our leadership.

One of the most dangerous temptations we face when we're working for someone else is passivity. If authority brings us a feeling of control, the lack of that authority makes us feel, acutely, our lack of control. And when I feel out of the loop, without any control over the plan, I tend to feel disconnected from the outcome. As much as being in control forces me to think deliberately about my decisions, feeling like I lack control causes me to do the opposite. When I feel like I'm being handed decisions, I throw my hands up, but not in the Taio Cruz kind of way. Worse, when I make decisions to move forward and those decisions get overturned by "those in charge," I tend to respond by sitting on my hands, passively.

The example that immediately comes to my mind in our organization is the preaching calendar. For those of you who preach, what would you say is the key ingredient to a great sermon series? If we can agree to set aside the power of God for a moment, I would argue that it's great planning. I've found that my best preaching happens when I've had time to let an idea simmer. Just like great pork butt, low and slow is the key. The further out I plan, the better I can prepare, and the more likely I am to cultivate life-changing, God-breathed principles and applications.

The challenge I face as a campus pastor is that Andy Stanley ultimately controls our preaching calendar. And don't misunderstand me; he should control it! He's the one preaching around thirty-five Sundays a year, the majority of our services. And even though he tries to plan ahead, sometimes the length of his series changes. A four-part series turns into a five-part series, and that turns my three-part series into a two-part series as the schedule changes and I adapt around him. If I'm not married to an idea, it's not usually a problem to change. But it can be frustrating and problematic when I've spent hours and hours planning and preparing for a three-part series only to find out a week beforehand that it's changed and I need to drop an entire message. As frustrating as that can be, the greatest temptation is for me to become passive about my planning for the next time. It's easier to just wait on the firm plan than to create firm ideas around a wobbly plan.

Maybe you don't have the authority you want. Or you're frustrated because your well-planned idea keeps getting shot down. Maybe you're discouraged because you feel like you've been labeled and it's keeping you from the opportunities you want. Well, "Don't let it beat cha." It wants to. If you don't pay attention to it, it will. Before you even realize it, the passivity of subordination will settle on you like the plague. That's why resisting passivity is the best response.

THE GENERATION OF CONTRADICTION

Every one of us is walking around carrying loads of messy contradictions. For starters, I know I'm a sinful wretched person; yet I also know that I am fully forgiven because of Jesus's work on the cross. Both are true and I walk around with the cognitive knowledge of both at the same time.

Growing up on the border of the millennial generation, I can relate to one of the common criticisms made of them: being known as the trophy generation. I received participation ribbons and was applauded by teachers, parents, and administrators for anything and everything. And like many twenty-somethings today, I grew up being told I could be anything I wanted. And I believed it. I grew up believing Shakespeare's line, "Why, then, the world's mine oyster, which I with sword will open."[1] And of course there will be a diamond-studded pearl inside. Everyone has told me for my whole life that thus is so.

Despite the criticism of receiving too much positive affirmation, there is a part of this I think is good. The sense of accomplishment and confidence it has built has created a generation of young leaders who are bold, confident, eager, and ambitious. Why wouldn't you go for it when you've been told your whole life you can do anything? Sometimes, you just start believing it. This thinking creates a courageous mindset that is willing to try things, audaciousness to go for gold, and boldness to bust through obstacles that have held previous generations back. I know it has created confidence in me. Maybe an over-confidence, but I'll let the sociologists arm wrestle over that one.

The contradiction that many point out with the millennial generation is that even though we're highly confident, we're also deeply risk averse for some reason. The parents who have done all the handholding haven't helped this generation move ahead on their own. When your parent does your homework, you get a great grade, which is nice. And it might help you get into a better college, but it teaches you that you don't really have a risk of failing.

As much as we laugh at it, trying to keep kids overly safe, avoiding failing or falling, has its own consequences. My friend Dr. Tim Elmore says that the removal of monkey bars on playgrounds is perhaps the clearest example of this. The monkey bars teach us something about controlling our bodies, learning to take calculated risks, and still avoid the nasty falls. Even though there is always the potential for an injury, a child who learns to play on the monkey bars experiences that feeling of accomplishment that most other pieces of playground equipment cannot provide. Taking away the monkey bars has led to the walking contradiction we see in this risk-averse, overconfident generation of young leaders.

I see the contradiction in my own life, and I bet you do too. So, what do we do about it? Awareness is a great first step. Learn to recognize that a low risk tolerance may be resulting in passivity in your leadership. In the poetically poignant movie *Tommy Boy*,[2] Ray Zalinksy, played by Dan Aykroyd, offers a fantastically helpful piece of advice to Tommy, played by Chris Farley. Tommy steps onto an elevator with Ray and within just a few moments, Ray detects an unusual odor coming from Tommy. Without making eye contact, Ray says with a strong Midwestern accent, "Went a little heavy on the pine tree perfume there, kid?"

Tommy sheepishly replies, "Sir, it's a taxicab air freshener."

I love the brilliant retort by Ray. "Good. You've pinpointed it. Step two is washing it off."

Obviously, there is nothing helpful about passivity when leading others. Anyone who has created anything has done it through intentionality. Even those who try and fail gain the benefit of an opportunity for learning. Thomas Edison is credited for saying, "I didn't fail. I just found 2,000 ways not to make a light bulb." The greatest danger of not being in charge and waiting around until you are, is that you never learn to risk or fail and how to handle that experience. You never learn from those mistakes. Learn to recognize that low-level fear in you that says, "If you try and fail, you'll get labeled as someone who can't." Learning to ignore that voice is crucial. So being aware of passivity is the first step, but step two is learning to reject it and take action.

WHEN WAITING DOESN'T WORK

There's a value in our organization we call *remaining open-handed*. This is massively important for us because we know that a team filled with closefisted people will become toxic. The best teammates are those who are willing to share ideas, who are able to withstand their idea not being used, and who understand when they're asked to carry something outside of their job description for a season. That's remaining openhanded.

The danger of this value is that we begin to create leaders who lack the intentionality to fight passiveness. We've all worked with people who were too hesitant to take on more responsibility. Instead, they wait for direction. Maybe they hesitate for fear that their intentionality will be perceived as a land grab. Maybe they hesitate for fear of mishandling the responsibility. Maybe they hesitate out of laziness or because they're already overwhelmed with their current load.

Hoping someone will hand you responsibility may not be helping your boss. If you truly want to be a leader who is leading when you're not in charge and capable of being trusted with more, you have to be willing to add responsibilities to your current role. When you sense yourself standing around waiting for more, a great first step is to look around for things that no one is addressing and take the first step. Don't play the waiting game. You'll miss opportunities to lead.

A few years ago, a young leader who worked for me would end every one-on-one meeting by telling me he had margin for more responsibility. I thought his job was flush with responsibility, but obviously, it wasn't keeping him busy enough. He wanted more, and told me so . . . on the regs (that means with regularity for those of you who can't handle my abbrevs). To his credit, at least he was honest about it.

With the best of intentions, he would tell me, "What's on my plate is not completely keeping me busy and I've got more to give. If there's anything else you need me to do, let me know." While I appreciated the sentiment, I finally had to tell him that I needed him to be more intentional about picking up responsibilities. I told him he'd be most helpful if he could find problems that needed to be solved. I needed him using his additional margin to add value to what we were trying to accomplish. Part of his job was to find ways within his area of responsibility to make better what we were trying to accomplish. That was *his* job, not my job.

When you wait for your boss to tell you what to do, your boss then has to think about how to do their job *and* your job. If you're always waiting to be handed more responsibility or a new opportunity, you'll likely become someone who can't be handed anything of importance. On our team, the people I trust most are the ones handling the most and taking the initiative to find and solve the problems I haven't even noticed yet. So if you're not busy, get busy! A waiting posture doesn't win in the long run. If you don't know where to start, look around. There are always responsibilities, projects, processes, products, or even people who are underutilized that others around you are just not noticing.

ACTIONS YOU CAN ALWAYS TAKE

Two years ago, my life changed radically. I'm not sure why it took so long, but for some reason, it wasn't until age thirty-four that it finally clicked for me. I finally decided no one else could fix or ruin my life. That's my job. Granted, I was in the middle of a pretty substantial job transition, but the change happened because I decided to quit playing defense and start playing offense. Every person is either on one side or the other. There are those who are deciding what kind of person they want to be and those who are simply responding to what life is handing them.

We may have every intention of being in the first group, but it takes more than just intention. I decided that to be the leader I wanted to be, I had to quit responding to life and instead get out in front by developing *better daily habits*. I decided to wake up earlier, become more consistent in doing what I said I valued most, and spend more time preparing for the day ahead. I became convinced I didn't have to be in charge to take charge.

When I'm not in charge, I feel like I have no control and feel forced to be reactive.

Reactivity perpetuates passivity.

Passivity causes me to feel stuck.

If you feel stuck in your job, you don't have to stay stuck. Instead of getting caught in the passivity cycle, I want to give you a road map to resuscitate your proactivity. There are habits you can cultivate to help you reject passivity: choosing, planning, and responding. And they're more than another slick three-letter memory aid. If you do this CPR, it can bring your leadership skills back to life.

Choosing

To get out of the passivity cycle, it's going to take some initiative. You simply need to choose something—anything—that you will pick up and own.

In my early twenties, I was in a season of going from one internship to another. During that season, just about every internship included some kind of closet I had to clean out. I now realize that in every church or organization, or even a home for that matter, there is *that* closet that just accumulates all of the junk. When you don't know what to do with something, you just throw it in that closet. In most organizations, there is a day that comes around every year, coincidentally right around the time interns begin working, when the closet needs to be cleaned out.

Now that I'm on the other side of the closet-cleaning equation, I love seeing interns that choose to clean it out before being asked. Every organization has closets like this. The closet *represents that thing that needs to be done, but no one wants to do.* There are projects, problems, and processes that get neglected. They may have worked once, but over time were forgotten or abandoned. During a crisis season some things were dropped and never picked up again. Often, these are the long-term planning items, the practices and habits that make an organization healthy over the long run. But they will take some work to clean out and polish off.

I believe a natural way to reject passivity is to focus on that closet. Choose a closet to clean. Find something that no one else wants to do and just handle it. Find that thing that is always brought up in meetings but no one ever does anything about, and go find a solution for it or choose to own it in a way that a great leader would!

I didn't see these types of things as opportunities until I started to move up in leadership and away from the front lines of ministry. But the truth is that the closer you are to the action, the more insight you have on what needs to change at that micro level. You will likely have better insight than your boss does as to the changes needed for the day-to-day processes that make up your job and those of your coworkers. You're closer to it. The manager at Waffle House isn't going to know how to make a waffle taste better; the cook at Waffle House will. When I talk to interns or entry-level team members who feel they can't make a difference, I get giddy, explaining to them that they are perfectly positioned to be able to see what most needs to change. In fact, no one is better positioned to see what isn't working. So find something that needs to change, choose to own it, and come up with a realistic plan to fix it.

One of the people in our organization whom I know does this best is Robby Angle. While I was at Browns Bridge Church (part of North Point Ministries), we hired Robby as a middle school groups director. It's not a very sexy title, but it's a crucial role for our ministry to middle school students. The job description for that role is twofold. First, he needs to ensure that adult volunteer small group leaders have everything they need to lead the students to discover a faith of their own. Second, he needs to remove any obstacles in their way. Robby has a business degree from the University of Florida and a master's degree in counseling from Appalachian State. He has also led post-earthquake relief efforts for an entire country in southeast Asia. Needless to say, he was feeling bored in his role after about ten months because he was crushing it!

Here's what I love, though. Instead of getting frustrated with what he couldn't do because of the level of his role, Robby started looking around to find ways to make stuff better. That's what great leaders do. Having spent a few years after graduate school counseling teenagers, he was already convinced that the way to help a student best is to involve the student's father. So after he had competently mastered the core essentials of his role, he asked if anyone on the team had a problem with him tinkering with ways to help facilitate better relationships between fathers and sons. What he came up with was not rocket science, but it was well thought out, carefully orchestrated, and manageable through our existing small group model.

Robby created an event for fathers to give their eighth-grade sons a blessing before they entered high school. He called the event a pig roast, because what's not to love about a bunch of fathers and sons roasting a pig in an open field? After massive amounts of pork were consumed, everyone was directed to the small groups they had been involved with for the past three years. Each father had been instructed to write a one-page letter to his son, explaining in detail why he was proud of him. As you can imagine, after those letters were read, there wasn't a dry eye to be found. This event has now been implemented at all of our campuses and it is seen as one of the key milestones for our students.

And it all happened because one guy decided to lead when he wasn't in charge by choosing to take initiative. If you can find ways to add value in the areas others are looking to avoid, you will find yourself with more on your plate than you could ever ask for. What is not getting the energy or focus it needs? What are the things that continuously come up in meetings but never become to-dos for anyone on your team? What are the things you can pick up that others have put down? Decide to be the one who isn't afraid to pick it up and choose to own what others are looking to avoid. That's the first step in rejecting passivity. Make a choice.

Planning

Another antidote for passivity is developing the margin to plan. The whirlwind of your calendar likely has a way of whipping you into submission, but great leaders, whether they're in charge or not, make room for planning. Instead of reacting to your calendar, create margin to get out in front of it. I mentioned earlier that lacking time to plan and prepare for meetings is a common problem for me. When that happens, I resort to the easiest, least resistant plan. And having no plan is a plan in and of itself. When you're living meeting to meeting, you're being reactive instead of proactive.

Here is how planning will help you counter passivity in your leadership. *The most well-planned idea usually wins the meeting.* Think about the last several meetings you've sat in where you had to make a decision about something. When the topic of the meeting is sent out ahead of time, there are usually one or two people who have done a bit of homework, research, and planning to determine what they are going to share. I've noticed that the most thoroughly baked idea is most often the dish chosen for the menu. It doesn't mean it's the best idea, but it's the idea that went the furthest down the road. But coming to a meeting prepared takes a little bit of planning.

Last December, I had the opportunity to attend a football practice for the University of Alabama as they prepared for the College Football Playoffs. It took some explanation for Jenny to understand why I would spend time doing this, but I convinced her that anytime I get the opportunity to see one of the best practice their craft, I need to take it. While I was at the practice, I met Jeff Allen, the head football athletic trainer for the team. Jeff has the daunting task of sitting in staff meetings with Nick Saban, having to give an account of the injured players.

After some casual conversation, I asked Jeff, "When a new staff member steps onto your team, what do you tell them is the key to working for Coach Saban?" Without any hesitation, Jeff responded, "Have a plan. If a player has an injury, don't just tell Coach Saban about the injury. Be prepared to propose a plan on what you're doing to rehabilitate the player." He then went into a hypothetical explanation. "If a player has a hamstring injury, I can't just say, 'Yeah, Coach. Jalen has a pulled hamstring. We're still trying to figure it out.' Instead, I need to say, 'Coach, Jalen has a hamstring injury and we've gotten these two doctors to give us opinions on the severity of it. And here is the plan that we're moving forward with to get healthy.'"

This is a key idea to remember for your own work: *never present your boss with just a problem*. Always bring a plan for the solution. But remember, it takes planning to come up with a plan. Where in your calendar can you begin to make room to plan? I don't know Jeff's weekly schedule, but it's clear he has found a way to create margin in his calendar for planning. Planning takes time, thought, and mental space to be able to think through solutions. In my calendar, I've found that the only time to do this is early in the morning. On most workdays, whether I have something due or not, I'm up early working through my list of what's most important for the day, the week, and the next ninety days. I'm at my best when I'm planning well in the margins of my calendar. And you should plan time to plan in the margins of your calendar.

Responding

Many people who have an ambition to coach sports desire to be the head coach. Most people don't set their sights on being an assistant for life. However, most of the great head coaches were great assistant coaches. The last few winning Super Bowl coaches spent a good portion of their careers as assistants. Bill Belichick was an assistant for twelve years with the New York Giants, mostly under Bill Parcels. Before Gary Kubiak won the Super Bowl with the Denver Broncos, he cut his coaching teeth as an assistant with the San Francisco 49ers, winning a Super Bowl as a quarterback coach in 1994. Pete Carroll was an assistant for almost twenty years before he stepped into the head coaching role. Being a good assistant is key to learning to be the head coach.

To be a great assistant coach, you have to be able to anticipate and respond to what's important to the head coach. The assistant coach has to move one step ahead during practice, setting up the next drill in order to keep practice moving. Leaders seeking to resist the passivity of not being in control need to do the same. Rather than responding only to what comes next on their calendars, great leaders respond to what's most important to the boss and move accordingly. In order to be able to anticipate and respond to the direction the boss is heading, you and I must know what is most important to who we're working for. Here are a few questions that can help if you're currently stuck in passivity:

- What has my boss established as the greatest "win" for our team?
- If your boss could wave a magic wand and have something done, what would it be?
- What is your boss most worried about? What is creating stress? How can you relieve that?
- On your team, what is a frequently discussed problem? Can you take steps toward fixing it today?

Word to the wise: make sure to ask these questions of yourself before you ask them of your boss.

As you train yourself to *choose* what's not getting done, *plan* time for future planning in the margins of your calendar, and then *respond* to what is most pressing for your boss, you'll have a game plan that can work. That's the CPR for resuscitating the proactivity that defeats passivity.

A WASTE OF TIME

Being under the authority of someone else often feels like waiting. But don't let waiting turn into passivity. Get out of the rut of passivity. Think differently. If you are in a season of waiting, what can you learn now that you can only learn from the seat you're in? Where can you cultivate influence with those around you, to learn how to serve them better? What new skill can you learn that you could only learn while you're in the position you're in? What's in the way of your team accomplishing more? What can you do to remove that obstacle?

When Moses was in Pharaoh's house, it wasn't a waste of time. He was becoming acquainted with what made those in Pharaoh's house tick, he was building influence with his Hebrew brothers and sisters, and he would eventually use all of this to free God's people.

When Joseph was in Potiphar's house and in prison, those days weren't a waste of time. He was learning to problem solve in ways he would use in an even greater context under Pharaoh. He was cultivating influence with those around him—those he would eventually lead.

When David was under Saul's leadership, that wasn't a waste of time. He was learning how to create an oasis of excellence with the military that he was in charge of. He was building relationships with those around him—not simply to be in charge of them, but to learn how to lead them well.

My good friend Tim Cooper has this line that pops into my head all the time: "You will never passively find what you do not actively pursue." You're not going to bump into leadership or wait your way into it. Don't let the feeling of having little control beat you. Find a way to initiate by choosing, planning, and responding to reject passivity. Make use of the time God has given you because what you're doing now matters greatly!

> You will never passively find what you do not actively pursue.
>
> TIM COOPER

PART 3

Challenging
Authority

CHAPTER 8

CHALLENGING UP

"Have you done yours?"

This was a question my parents asked me every day when I was a kid, and I hated it. My dad came up with it. He had some pretty strong beliefs about the value of studying. Every night, Sunday through Thursday, whether schoolwork was due or not, each of us had to sit at the desk in our respective bedroom and engage in an hour's worth of studying, reading, or homework. As I look back now, this strikes me as one of those ideas that parents employ in a moment of frustration, but rarely follow through with. Not my dad. He was committed to it. Every night, and I mean *every* night, homework or not, we would sit at our desks for one solid hour.

Though each of us had our own room, our house was not large. My room was adjacent to my younger sister's room and the wall we shared became an instrument for us to practice our own variation of Morse code. After years of perfecting our own tapping language, we decided enough was enough. We needed a better system of communication. And so we did what any prepubescent teenager would in that situation. Like Andy Dufresne in *The Shawshank Redemption*, we used our primitive tools—pens, rulers, and scissors—to cut a fist-sized hole through the drywall, effectively connecting my room with my sister's room. It was brilliant. The drive-through at the bank had a similar system, so we were convinced this remodel of the wall was adding to our home value. Quietly, covertly, and in unison, we dug out that hole.

Unfortunately, we weren't able to keep it quiet enough, and the sounds of our unauthorized construction project alerted my dad. He was not as excited about our improvement to the wall. I've seen him mad from time to time, but I don't remember him getting quite that hot before. In my mind, it seemed like such a small matter. But he was furious.

Now that I'm a homeowner myself and have experienced the frustration when my kids damage the property I'm responsible for, I understand his emotional state. But at the time, his anger befuddled me. What was he not getting? How could he not see that this was making our house better, more efficient? We had essentially just proved our brilliance and worth to him. In my mind, I was making our home better. I had found a problem and had come up with a solution to fix and improve it. Of course, I had no concept of ventilation or HVAC systems or electrical wiring, and I certainly knew nothing about "property damage." I just saw an opportunity, an area that needed improvement, and I did what was needed to make that happen.

CHALLENGED TO CHALLENGE

The instinct to do what needs to be done is an essential aspect of leadership. While the way I went about making the changes I felt needed to be made wasn't the greatest (it's usually best to get permission if you don't own something), that desire was not wrong.

Leaders see problems. They see things that aren't working. And they come up with solutions.

Leaders make a way when others can't find a way. Leaders look at what is, see what could be, and organize others to move toward the preferred future. Leaders are not rabble-rousers, but they will challenge the status quo. They are not okay with "this is the way we've always done it." They refuse to accept mediocrity. Leaders are not content to sit on the sidelines, managing a system that is yielding solid results, when there are potential changes pregnant with greater results. I say this because if you're bewildered or mystified by your boss's comfort with the way things are going, I want you to know that there is not something wrong with you. You have the instincts of a leader. You may be feeling the weight of what God has put in you, the desire to effect change and improve what isn't working.

Leadership can feel like a burden. I'm sure you've had moments where you would rather not feel the pressure of what could be—when you wish you could just turn off the drive for more, better, faster, or stronger. But when it's in you, it's in you. And if it weren't in you, you probably wouldn't be reading this book.

Without challenge, we do not change.

I don't know the specifics of your situation, but I know that something in your church or organization needs to change. Perhaps God has put that desire in you and has put you in your organization because it needs that change. But in order to see that change happen, you're going to have to challenge and you're going to have to challenge well.

As the authors of *The Leadership Challenge* put it, "Leaders must be agents of change."[1] It's motivating, freeing, confirming, and challenging all at the same time. But just knowing that doesn't mean it's any easier to determine how to do it in your organization. So this chapter is about how you do this. It's about the leader's responsibility to challenge well.

FREE AGENCY

Unless you're a fan of the Milwaukee Brewers or the Cleveland Indians, you probably missed this story. In August of 2016, Jonathan Lucroy, an All-Star catcher for the Brewers, refused to be traded to the Indians. That's it. That's the story: he refused to be traded. Lucroy said, "When you are dealing with life-changing, life-altering decisions like this, there are a lot of factors that come into play, mostly family. The other half of that is your future in this league and your career. There are a lot of different things to take in. Whenever those things don't line up, decisions have to be made that might be tough, but that's the way it has to be."[2] His decision was not all that popular among baseball fans.

Lucroy weighed the pros and cons of being traded from the Brewers, and in the end he made a decision that was best for his family. Now that's a pretty admirable statement about family, but it's also a reminder that putting your stakes in the ground on a decision might not be popular.

What Lucroy did to the Brewers reminds me of what Maura did to George Costanza on "The Strongbox"[3] episode of *Seinfeld*. George was dead set on breaking up with his girlfriend, Maura, but she was just not going to do it.

> **George:** Maura, I, uh—I want you to know . . . I-I've given this a lot of thought. I'm sorry, but . . . we, uh, we have to break up.

Maura: No.

George: What's that?

Maura: We're not breaking up.

George: W-we're not?

Maura: No.

George: (Pauses. Looks at his coffee.) All right.

How could you not love George Costanza?

Let's go back to Jonathan Lucroy, because there is more to his story than what I've shared. I want you to hear the rest of it. Because the real story is not the decision Lucroy made in 2016; it's the story behind that story. It's the story of a man named Curt Flood.

Curtis Charles Flood was born in Houston on January 18, 1938, but was raised in Oakland, California. He lived the dream of many young kids, playing professional baseball for fifteen years. He played for the St. Louis Cardinals in the 1960s, made three All-Star teams, won the Gold Glove for fielding for seven consecutive years, and batted over .300 for seven seasons. In 1964, he even led the National League in hits (211).

Then, in 1969, the St. Louis Cardinals included Flood in a seven-player trade to the Philadelphia Phillies. But Curt Flood said, "No, thank you." Flood didn't think he should be treated like a commodity, so he refused. In doing this, Flood became one of the most controversial figures in sports. His refusal created a legal firestorm. The case was eventually heard in front of the US Supreme Court, and it caused an earthquake that shook professional baseball to the core. Flood's courageous refusal to move challenged the status quo and created what is commonly known today as free agency.

Here is why Flood's decision was so controversial. At the time of Flood's trade refusal, teams owned the rights to players, and players were beholden to the team for life—even if they had fulfilled their contractual obligations. Flood equated this ownership and lack of freedom to slavery, saying, "I do not feel I am a piece of property to be bought and sold irrespective of my wishes. I believe that any system which produces that result violates my basic rights as a citizen and is inconsistent with the laws of the United States."[4] Flood held to his deep beliefs and strong convictions even though it was costly for him. He sat out the entire 1970 season. He received hate mail, death threats, lawsuits, had an IRS lien placed on his mother's home, and saw the bankruptcy of his business, Curt Flood Associates. Four years after Flood's refusal, though, the courts ruled in favor of the players and this case became the lynchpin for securing the rights of players, leading to the start of the free agency system.

Challenging the status quo is no walk in the park. Though few people have experienced the amount of resistance Curt Flood did, many have felt the collateral damage of challenging their boss on things that needed to change. And we know that there is a chasm between seeing a change that needs to be made and having the emotional intelligence to do it in a way that does not limit your career. Even a secure, healthy leader may bite back at you and respond defensively when he or she feels threatened by a challenge. How you handle this delicate issue matters. So why is it so difficult to challenge others well? I see three significant reasons.

Challenge brings change, and change is inherently challenging.

In *The Leadership Challenge*, Kouzes and Posner write, "Leaders must challenge the process precisely because any system will unconsciously conspire to maintain the status quo and prevent change."[5] Any challenge to the current system or process will require change, and the status quo resists change. In fact, healthy systems are often built with this in mind and are predictable in the midst of chaotic circumstances. And many systems can get quite good at withstanding challenges without changing. I've even noticed this about myself: the older I get, the more I resist change.

One of the reasons this is true is that I really like the way I see the world. My friend Rodney is one of the pastors at our church, and he thinks all of us are addicted to the way we see the world. I think he's right. It's as if we're intoxicated by the way we think, the way we do, the way we process. We are all attracted to opinions that validate the way we see life and we resist opinions that disagree with the way we see things. It's why people are committed to CNN and opposed to Fox News . . . or the other way around. Hearing opinions that differ from the way I see things feels like rejection, which is why I resist change. Hearing that I have a need for change is a form of rejection. You're telling me that something about me is wrong. It needs to go. And I don't like that.

There was a time in my life when change was the norm. I barely even noticed it or thought about it. This was also a time in my life when I didn't have much to my name. During my college years, I still drove that twenty-year-old white Volvo 240 DL I had picked up in high school. It was a tank. When I left college and headed to graduate school, I could literally fit everything I owned inside that Volvo—a collection of clothes, books, and CDs—remember those? I didn't own a bed, so I bought one at a garage sale when I arrived at seminary in Dallas. Now I'm in my midthirties, I live on a cul-de-sac, own a minivan, and my most beloved possession is the Charter Club 500-thread-count sheets on our king-size bed. I know what some of you are thinking: I've grown soft in my old age. Well, you're right. I have. And so have my sheets.

I bring all of that up because it's worth tucking away in the back of your mind. Challenging someone is threatening because it calls for change. And no matter who you are, change is not easy. All of us are in search of the path of least resistance, and when we find it, we cling to it like a box of Little Debbies. There is nothing wrong with you because you want to challenge the way things are done. It's quite normal for a leader to feel this drive. But there is nothing wrong with your boss either, just because she seems allergic to change. All of us have a sizeable magnet in us that pulls us toward the way things have always been done. Don't forget that. Recently, I saw a bumper sticker that said, "There are two things I hate: Change and the way things are." And your boss was driving the car.

The more personally your boss relates to his job, the more personally your boss will take your challenge.

Great leaders don't get defensive. Put that on your bulletin board. Unfortunately, all of us have been defensive about something we've been challenged about. If you haven't, it's going to happen. Just know that. And the more passionate and invested you are in the topic or position being challenged, the more personally you take the challenge. If you were to challenge me about the way I organize the files on my computer, I would say to you, "Have at it, homie! Make yourself comfortable. Feel free to sit in the driver's seat and go 'Martha Stewart' on my hard drive."

I don't take the organization of my hard drive very personally because I'm not passionate about it. It's a bit of a mess and I'm okay with it. I don't really care all that much.

But if you were to challenge the way I parent, or worse, the way my kids are behaving, I would instinctively and immediately, and mentally drop a pin on where I last saw my boxing gloves. I take parenting seriously. Hopefully my desire to

Great leaders don't get defensive.

learn and grow would kick in and help me listen to what you have to say, but your challenge would immediately put me on the defensive. It's natural that the more personally we take something, the more personal we'll be with anyone who challenges it.

Any change to the present system will be perceived as a criticism of past leadership.

One of the challenges of changing jobs is watching what your successor does in your vacated position. If they come in with a baseball bat, taking a swing at everything you put in place, it's difficult not to take offense to that. When you change something I put in place, it's easy for me to think, "Who does he think he is? We'll see how that goes, but I doubt it will work. I kind of hope it *doesn't* work." That's gross, I know. It's sinful, and I'm asking God to change this in my heart, but honesty is step one.

When I stepped into the campus pastor role at Browns Bridge Church, I didn't know what I was doing. That's not false humility. That's just honest truth. I had been in a youth pastor role for the previous five years and before that, I'd been in school for the last twenty years. I had a lot of head knowledge about the Bible and a lot of theories about doing ministry, but I had very little hands-on, practical experience. I was in that campus pastor role for about four years before I moved back to North Point, the original campus, to take a similar position there.

About a year after I moved into the campus pastor role at North Point, an odd thing happened. Because there had been some significant transitions at Browns Bridge Church over the years, Andy Stanley—my boss—decided to step into the role as their campus pastor. This was the same role I had just held for the previous four years. Now, all of a sudden, my boss is doing my previous job. And he was making a lot of changes. Of course, I watched him make those changes, and I questioned everything I had done. *Oh, that's what I should've been doing?* I thought. With every move he made, I felt more and more insecure as a leader. Every change felt like an indirect criticism of how I had been leading. Through much processing and inner dialogue, I came to the conclusion that every leader does what seems right to them in the moment. As easy as it was for his changes to feel like criticisms, I couldn't let his changes be an indictment of what I had done.

If I felt indirectly criticized by his changes, I'm guessing other leaders I've worked for could have felt indirectly criticized by changes I've made. When a leader is feeling criticized by change, it doesn't mean they are a leader driven solely by insecurity. Just know and assume that most leaders struggle with feeling indirectly criticized by change. Put yourself in that position. Wouldn't you perceive changes to a system you've put in place and led for years as a criticism of your past leadership? When you challenge what *is*, others perceive that as a criticism of who *was*. This doesn't mean you shouldn't challenge. It just means you need to understand how it might feel to be challenged, and be sure to communicate with that in mind.

Knowing that "challenging up" and raising questions about the status quo is difficult does not change the fact that you should do it when necessary. But it may change how you do it. It can inform your timing, the way you approach the topic and present your challenge, and the tone of your voice as you share. Don't underestimate the power of awareness; it's first aid for ignorance. Remember what G.I. Joe taught us in the eighties: "Now you know. And knowing is half the battle."

THE CHICK-FIL-A MILKSHAKE

We all have our kryptonite—the thing that, without fail, has our number. For me it's the milkshake. My favorite milkshake is from Ivanhoes in Upland, Indiana. As The Notorious B.I.G. said, "If you don't know, now you know." Upland is in the middle of nowhere, but if you're ever near it, it's worth stopping at Ivanhoes. Right up there on my list and slightly more accessible to most people would be the cookies and cream milkshake from Chick-fil-A. As a clergyman and resident of metro Atlanta, I have taken an oath to love Chick-fil-A until I die. But I don't take that oath as an obligation. It's an honor and a joy to carry. I really love everything about Chick-fil-A. Our church is better in so many ways simply because of our proximity to the headquarters of one of the most service-minded, open-handed, and successful organizations on planet earth.

The bread-and-butter of this Monday through Saturday quick-service restaurant is the Chick-fil-A chicken sandwich, but their milkshake is one of the better milkshakes you'll find. In 2008, just two years after it was launched, the milkshake was the highest rated product on their menu. But did you know that the Chick-fil-A milkshake almost didn't come to be? It's crazy, I know. The story of how it came about is a fantastic case study on the power of learning how to "challenge up."

Shane Todd was the pioneer of the Chick-fil-A milkshake. A product as significant and as successful as Chick-fil-A's milkshake can never be credited to a single person. But if you were to ask most people in and around Chick-fil-A, they will gladly credit Shane as the key driver for the innovation and evolution of the milkshake. Shane is a franchise owner and operator in Athens, Georgia. If you're not familiar with Chick-fil-A's franchise model, I'll give you a quick primer. Chick-fil-A uses an unusual, atypical franchise model for fast-food restaurants, where the corporate organization maintains ownership of the store. Because there is such direct corporate involvement, it leads to a healthy tension for someone like Shane. He is both an employee of Chick-fil-A and he has an ownership mindset for his own local store. As a leader, Shane is entrepreneurial, driven, and innovative. He's not content with just managing a local restaurant but is constantly looking for new ideas in new markets to introduce at his local Chick-fil-A.

Long before the milkshake was launched nationwide in the spring of 2006, customers were already asking for another dessert option. Shane's own store was receiving multiple requests for milkshakes. The common thought at Chick-fil-A's central office was that it would take too long for them to provide a quality product without slowing down the high-quality, quick service the store was committed to providing. According to Woody Faulk, who was the vice president of menu strategy at the time, the milkshake project had been going in circles at headquarters. Things were now at a standstill.

Despite some red flags from the product development team, Shane began covertly testing a milkshake in his store. He was determined to prove to Woody Faulk and others that this was an offering they could make to improve customer satisfaction, and it could be done quickly. And so the great milkshake experiment began at his store in Athens, Georgia. Shane and his team personally bought the ingredients needed to transform the ice cream that Chick-fil-A was already serving into a quality milkshake that customers liked. After tinkering with the product and training his employees how to prepare it, the team in Athens discovered a creative way to serve a delicious tasting milkshake while keeping the order times short. With very little marketing, word of the milkshake began to spread throughout Athens. Within a few months, Shane's store was selling hundreds of milkshakes every day. They had avoided setting off any major alarms at the corporate offices, and the Athens store had created an even greater need for a new product. It was clear that customers wanted milkshakes. And Shane's team had proved it could be done.

The "make-it-or-break-it" moment for Shane's team came when Tim Tassopoulos, senior vice president of operations, decided to drop in to see what all the fuss was about. Tim was the decision maker. He could say yes or no to their little trial. But Shane was ready for Tim's visit. Like an old western gun fast draw, Shane challenged Tim to make two diet cokes faster than he could make a milkshake. If Shane couldn't make the milkshake fast enough, the trial was over. If he could, Tim would agree to allow the milkshake sales to continue. Guess who won?

I had the opportunity to talk with both Shane and Woody about this experience, and I've summarized a few of the leadership lessons I gleaned from Shane's attempt to challenge up the Chick-fil-A corporate hierarchy to see his milkshake vision become a reality at every restaurant.

Great leaders challenge up with the best motives. Shane wasn't innovating for innovation's sake. In fact, he wasn't all that concerned about getting credit for his innovation. His motive for wanting a milkshake on the menu was more altruistic: "At Chick-fil-A, we're all about serving our customers. If a customer wants a milkshake, I was determined to figure out how to provide one, because I want to serve that customer."

Great leaders are keenly aware of what the boss is most interested in. When possible, position your challenge as a step toward a greater solution for the macro-problem your boss is looking to solve. During this season, there was a massive customer service initiative by Chick-fil-A's president, Dan Cathy, about what they were calling "second-mile service." Instead of positioning the milkshake as a new product, Shane talked about the milkshake as a way to provide second-mile service to customers.

Great leaders know what's core and what's peripheral. And they police themselves accordingly. Shane seemed well aware of the boundaries of new product development for Chick-fil-A. Shane prefaced our conversation by saying, "If this were a burger, we would have never tried it. We would try sweet potato fries, but we would never try a burger. That's too far from our core offering. But because we already offered ice cream, this was just a derivation of what we were already providing our customers."

Great leaders challenge up quietly, but they are not silent. They know how, when, and with whom to communicate when trying something new. Woody Faulk was quick to compliment Shane on how well he communicated about the experiment he was trying. If Shane had told too many people, the pilot would have been shut down. If Shane had been completely silent, he would not have garnered the favor with key leaders that aided his project. In Woody's words, Shane wasn't silent, but he communicated like a submarine. Because of the great relationship Shane had built with Woody early in the process, Woody became an advocate and was able to play interference with some of the leaders within the organization who had doubts about the milkshake.

Here's the takeaway: if you've never had the Chick-fil-A milkshake, you've got to try it. And as you are enjoying that tasty treat, let it remind you of the power you have to challenge up. Existing paradigms can change, but it takes wisdom, patience, and the right strategy. You don't need authority, but you will need influence. You don't have to be the one in charge to shift the paradigm and challenge the status quo. You can do it from the seat you're sitting in right now, but you must still learn to challenge *well*.

A BRIDGE OR A WALL

Whether you're trying to create a new product like the Chick-fil-A milkshake or just wanting to change a system, idea, process, or tradition, challenging up requires a bridge of relationship that is strong enough to handle the weight of the challenge. Shane had the relational capital to make this withdrawal. Before you set out to challenge, you need to assess whether you've put in the work of relationship and if that relationship can bear the weight of the challenge you want to bring.

Here's how it works. You see something that is befuddling. *Why in the world do we do that?* It makes no sense to you, and you've often wondered why it hasn't been changed or challenged. You talk it over with some of your peers. You formulate a game plan. You nail down an approach to bring it up. From your perspective, the change makes total sense. And you assume your boss will see it that way as well.

The words you use when you share your idea are bricks that will either build a bridge of relationship for your idea or a wall of distrust. Since words matter, here are a few common statements and phrases you should probably avoid. This will likely require some self-control. But think about them like bricks. In what you say, are you building that bridge or are you putting up a wall?

Constantly comparing your team, organization, or church to another team, organization, or church

"Well, that church splits their middle school and high school programs."

"It just seems like that organization is always doing something more creative with their graphics than we are."

"Have you seen their website? It's way easier to navigate than ours."

Chances are, there is a church or organization doing something better than what you're doing. And that might even be the source of your desire to change and grow and improve. There is nothing wrong with that. In fact, you should keep your eyes open to what's happening in culture and what's working in other organizations to foster learning and growth. But constantly comparing your church to another church is like comparing your spouse to a former relationship. It never goes well.

Emphatically declaring that what you're doing now isn't working

"Our small groups just don't work. It's basically social hour for everyone involved."

"Kids don't learn anything in our environments."

Is there a better way to do what you're currently doing? Possibly. Is the idea you have for change a better way to approach the problem? Maybe so. However, definitive statements shut down conversation. They reveal a lack of empathetic thinking, which will ultimately build a wall and not a bridge. When someone is reckless with definitive statements, it reveals a lack of discernment and creates distance in relationships. The truth is that what you're currently doing, though probably flawed, is still working at some level. There are better ways to build your case than to speak with absolute certainty about what is currently happening. It immediately invalidates the work others are doing and questions your credibility.

Blaming the current situation on anyone, especially your boss

"This new registration system for check-in wasn't thought through. It's as if no one was paying attention to it."

"No one on our team feels like they can speak up. Maybe you shouldn't be a part of the meeting."

Any new idea is naturally going to challenge the status quo. When you raise that new idea, you will be implicitly blaming the status quo and all of its problems on those currently in charge. Adding to that with additional statements of blame will only damage the relationship and show them you aren't a team player and cannot be trusted. You may not directly blame someone for why something is not working, but you still want to avoid statements that imply blame or would lead your boss to question whether you have a particular individual in mind. You want to challenge with enough emotional intelligence to avoid blaming someone for what's currently being done.

Obstinately offering an ultimatum for your future

"I just don't know if I'll be able to make it here if you don't allow us to make this change."

"If I don't get the budget for that, I'm just not sure I can pull off the event."

Statements like these might be true. You may not be able to survive in a culture that doesn't allow for change. You might not be able to survive in an organization that is not willing to pay for the work or ministry it is expecting from you. You may not be able to keep your team motivated when the "they" is constantly squeezing every ounce of potential out of every opportunity. But ultimatums will rarely help you. An ultimatum eventually undermines your own leadership. Other leaders have led under far more stressful situations. Other leaders have done more with less. Other leaders have made work what you're saying will not work. Instead of using an ultimatum to effect change, convince your boss that you are on the same team, that you are behind him or her. Make sure your boss is aware of your perspective and explore together what the implications are if the decision is or is not made. Include them in the process of evaluating, rather than presenting specific choices or actions as foregone conclusions if immediate action is not taken.

WORTH THE RISK

I know you have a burden for change. You should! And we all know that if you do not raise the challenge, there will be no change. Challenging your leader or your boss is a risk. But without the risk, there are no rewards. Remember: how well you challenge will determine how much you change.

I grew up with this quote on the wall in my childhood bedroom. I read it a thousand times, but it only became personal when I decided to be courageous enough to make a change in my own life. Paul William "Bear" Bryant said, "If you believe in yourself and have dedication and pride—and never quit—you'll be a winner. The price of victory is high but so are the rewards."[6]

Victory is not just the change that takes place because you challenge up and lead when you aren't the one in charge. The victory is also the growth that takes place when you enter this process of learning as a leader. God has grown me more through the *process* of challenging my bosses than just about anything else at work. I've prayed more, found more humility, developed more courage, and allowed God to build my confidence in him because of these moments of challenge.

And hopefully you're still with me, because this is such an important aspect of leading when you aren't in charge. We're going to take one more chapter to look at what it means to challenge up. In the next chapter, I'll unpack the four most essential ingredients to the art of doing this well.

CHAPTER 9

BREAKING
DOWN
CHALLENGING
UP

Every once in a while, I'll prepare some kind of food dish and post it to social media. In theory, I disagree with the practice of posting pictures of food. Honestly, I think we're going to look back as a society at the insanity of everyone posting about food and we'll see it for the absurdity that it truly is. But until then, I'll admit I'm as guilty as anyone. I don't like it about myself, but yes, I'm a food-photo-poster. Too often, I think to myself before posting, "Ehrma ghertness. That looks delicious. Everyone needs to see this."

Naturally, someone will say to me, "Oh, I didn't know you like to cook." The comment always strikes me as odd, because I don't consider myself someone who likes to cook. I bake. I grill. I don't really *cook*. And I don't really bake or grill because I *like* baking or grilling. I do enjoy it, but that's not why I do it. I bake and I grill because of one simple reason: I love food. That might be an understatement. I have an obsession with dessert and meat. Something feels unhealthy about eating food as a hobby. But if

I'm honest, eating is a hobby for me. I enjoy it as a pleasure. I enjoy it as a pastime. I think that constitutes a hobby.

The more I dabble in the kitchen, the more I have come to see the importance of quality ingredients. A few years ago, I spent every weekend for a significant number of months searching for the best chocolate chip cookie. I honestly think I've found it. It has everything: crispy on the outside, soft in the middle, high ratio of chocolate to dough, and a pinch of salt on the top. What I've found is that there are certain ingredients that just can't be off-brand and shouldn't be skimped in quality or quantity. For instance, if the cacao percentage in the chocolate is not sixty percent at a minimum, I'm out. And if you would like to disagree with me, I'm willing to fight. This is real, people.

In a similar way (and potentially less violent because I'm not going to blows over these), there are some ingredients in the practice of challenging up that cannot be skimped. You can't cheat by using the cheap stuff or fake your way through this. Don't try to replicate it with something less than authentic. These ingredients are essential, and they cannot simply be marked off of a checklist. They need to be constantly checked and monitored. They ebb and flow depending on the situation and the people involved. And if you find you're lacking one of these ingredients, don't try challenging up without it. Each one is a learned skill, something you can practice, and each one is an area where you can continue to grow.

THE RELATIONSHIP

As I mentioned last chapter, when you decide to challenge up, nothing is more important than the relationship you have with the person you're challenging. Before you decide to approach your boss or even someone in another department with something potentially challenging, you need to think through the relationship you have with them. Do you get the sense they like you? Do you feel they respect you? Do they trust you?

And what about the other side of the equation? Do you like them? Do you respect them? Do they feel like you care about them? Maybe the most important question to think through before you move forward is this one: do you love your boss? You don't necessarily need to *like* your boss. You might not be buddies. You might not choose to hang with them on the weekends. But you need to choose to love your boss. Loving your boss means you genuinely want what's best for them and you're trying to do what's in their best interests.

Even though 1 Corinthians 13 is widely known as the Love Chapter, I find Philippians 2 to be extremely helpful in understanding what it looks like to love someone well. Philippians 2:3–4 reads like this: "Do nothing out of selfish ambition or vain conceit. Rather, in humility value others above yourselves, not looking to your own interests but each of you to the interests of the others." In other words, put yourself to the side. Choose what's important to the other person as more important than what's important to you. The other person is not more important than you, but act as if they are. If you have to make a decision between what's best for you and what's best for the other person, go with the latter. Obviously, this is not intuitive, and it's certainly not easy. It doesn't always mean doing exactly what the other person wants or asks you to do. In fact, the apostle Paul gives us a little secret toward motivation and inspiration. If you want to know exactly what it looks like to do this well, whether you're trying to love your boss, or anyone else for that matter, Paul gives us this insight in Philippians 2:5–8:

> In your relationships with one another, have the same mind-set as Christ Jesus:
>
>> Who, being in very nature God,
>>> did not consider equality with God something to be used
>>>> to his own advantage;
>>> rather, he made himself nothing by taking the very nature
>>>> of a servant,
>>> being made in human likeness.
>> And being found in appearance as a man,
>>> he humbled himself
>>> by becoming obedient to death—
>>>> even death on a cross!

Jesus had every right to demand that everyone cater to his interests, but he didn't do that. He had every right to take advantage of others for his sake, but he refused. He was and is valued above others, but he treated others as though they were more important. Instead of elevating himself, he poured himself out on behalf of others. He did what was best for others even when it cost him something—ultimately, his life.

Paul is saying that when you're not sure you can love someone else more than yourself, look to Jesus. Follow his lead. Take your cues from him. In every relationship, make sure the other person is convinced of these simple truths: "I am not in this relationship for me. I am in this for you." That's love. And to lead well as you are relating to your boss, you have to choose to love your boss this way. If you don't, challenging up won't work.

I cannot overemphasize how important this is. Leadership is not simply a matter of authority. Leadership is about influence. And challenging up is a form of leadership. You are leading your boss to make a decision that they might not make on their own. Choosing to love your boss is imperative if you're trying to lead your boss. You cannot lead someone well if you don't love them. Loving someone and leading them are a package deal. You can't have one without the other.

So let's say you know exactly what needs to change and you know exactly what you would like to challenge, but the relationship you have with your boss is weak. What should you do? I would suggest waiting and working on the relationship instead.

Be convinced that God put your boss in their position. Whether you like your boss or not, God establishes authority. We've spent most of this book looking at how to lead when you don't have the formal authority to do so, but don't take from this that authority is bad or useless. God created the channels of authority and God works through authority. It's pretty clear that God is a fan of authority. God builds life under and around authority, so don't buck against what God builds around. It's a bad idea, and it just doesn't work. The more convinced you are that God has appointed the authorities over you, the more responsible you will be with how you challenge them.

One of the greatest difficulties in challenging up is learning to challenge the process without appearing to challenge the person. Challenging someone personally always puts that person on his or her heels and creates an obstacle in the way of a mutually beneficial conversation. Being convinced that God establishes authority will allow you to challenge up without the sense that you're challenging them as a person.

To build trust, practice faithfulness. Nothing will win your boss over like selfless faithfulness over an extended period of time. If you don't yet feel like your boss trusts you because you haven't done enough to build that trust, waiting is not wasted. Sometimes it just takes more time to show your manager that you are not in it for yourself. Do the little things to build trust. Show that you are faithful with a little so you can be trusted with a little more.

Our high school pastor at North Point has done this better than anyone I've ever met. When Darren Youngstrom stepped into his job, he had a hill to climb. Because the entire staff had turned over, many volunteers and students quit attending after losing the connection to the former leader. Darren's first year on the job looked like failure after failure after failure. Every month, the dashboard of metrics we use to measure growth was telling a sad tale. A few of our more senior leaders felt like it was unrecoverable. They questioned whether he was cut out for the job.

I've noticed that too often, when things aren't going well for someone, our instinct is to look for more weakness in that person to justify the judgment we have made in our minds. Unfortunately, it just makes matters worse and makes it even more difficult to turn the momentum around. However, I've watched Darren turn it around. It didn't happen overnight, but slowly, he started winning others over through his faithfulness. I watched him pick up tasks that no one else wanted to pick up. He volunteered for weddings, funerals, baptisms, and tricky pastoral situations that many people dodge. He consistently delivered strong leadership in some difficult situations. And soon, the department he was responsible for began to grow. Volunteers started to buy in and so did our senior leadership. Over time, his faithfulness built trust.

Bring up disagreements when emotions are low. Jenny and I have learned that the best time to teach our kids how to obey is when the emotions are low and the consequences for disobedience are small. When the tensions are high, like when we're rushing to get out the door or we're stressed from a long day, that is not the best time to teach a child why obedience is so important. When it's Saturday afternoon, one of those rare moments when life is on chill mode, we'll have obedience practice. "Hey Lucy, let's practice. Show me how you can go put your shoes where they should go." And then when she does it, we dance like Justin Timberlake just asked us to be in the Tennessee Kids.

I wouldn't try obedience practice with your boss, but I do find it helpful to employ a similar idea. When emotions are low and we're speaking in hypotheticals, I've found it helpful to ask my boss this simple question, "Hey, this rarely happens, but I'm sure it will. When I disagree with something I see, what's the best way to bring that up with you?" It's amazing how disarming that question can be. Most people are aware that every human being is going to disagree with something from time to time. This question signals to your boss that you are thinking about those times. When you do have something you would like to challenge, you've already asked for permission and agreed upon the best way to handle that.

Champion publicly. Challenge privately. Over and over again, I've made the mistake of challenging the status quo in the wrong context and sabotaging my future ability to create change. Again, put yourself in your boss's shoes. When you're at your worst and someone questions or challenges you publicly, how does it make you feel? Embarrassed. Incompetent. Inadequate. What does it do to the relationship with that person? It plants seeds of doubt that you can't trust him, that she's not for you, and that he may even be out for your job.

The opposite is true when others champion us publicly. We feel built up, believed in, and pushed forward because of a public affirmation. It's powerful. And sure, if we were more secure, we could handle anyone at any time confronting or challenging what we've built, but we're not all that secure. We're all fragile in different ways. Choosing to champion your boss publicly is always a win. It builds a strong bridge, which can then handle the weight of challenging up. When you are ready to have that challenging conversation, the environment where you talk is also important. If you've put in the time, built trust with your boss, and championed him publicly, you might be able to challenge him in real time as something comes up or in a meeting with others. Most often, though, the conversation needs some blocked-off, dedicated, personal time.

In our organization, managers are expected to have routine one-on-ones with their team members. If you don't have a regular one-on-one with your boss, maybe it means you need to request a time for the two of you to sit down and talk. The more challenging the conversation, the more private it should be. Challenge privately. Champion publicly. Do not confuse these two! Though they sound similar, very little does more to damage a relationship than confusing them.

YOUR POSTURE

Another essential ingredient when you challenge up is your posture. Sit up! Sit straight! Your physical posture is defined as the way your body is positioned when you are sitting or standing. If you haven't seen Amy Cuddy's TED Talk entitled, "Your Body Language Shapes Who You Are,"[1] you need to see it. It's fascinating and quite hilarious as well.

Though your physical posture is important, when I talk about the posture of a leader, I'm thinking more about your nonphysical posture. How do you position yourself? How do you carry yourself? Your physical posture is important, but your non-physical or *emotional* posture is just as important, if not more so. Your *emotional* posture is determined by the thoughts and feelings you allow yourself to have toward yourself and your boss. Nothing affects your posture more than what you tell yourself about yourself and about your manager.

Choose to trust your boss. If you constantly dwell on how frustrated you are, you will go into your meetings feeling closed and negative. Those negative emotions, feelings, and thoughts will naturally leak out in what you say. And even if you guard your words, your boss will likely pick up on your nonverbal cues. For more on this, Markus Buckingham's chapter from *The One Thing You Need To Know: . . . About Great Managing, Great Leading, and Sustained Individual Success* is a must-read. Buckingham argues that the most common behavior in every great marriage is the decision to believe the best about the other person. He summarizes his advice with this directive: "Find the most generous explanation for each other's behavior and believe it."[2] This insight is congruent with what Paul says in 1 Corinthians 13:7 about love: "It always protects, always trusts, always hopes, always perseveres." Very little will influence your posture toward your boss more than choosing to trust your boss.

Trusting that your boss has your best interest in mind is a

choice. Unless you have seen mounds of evidence that your boss is unworthy, you must choose to trust. If your trust is broken, talk to someone about how you are feeling and seek advice on how to respond. Otherwise, choose to trust your boss. It will not only help your boss, it will help you as well. And choosing to trust your boss builds trust with your boss. You've felt this yourself if you've had someone report to you. This is also one of the more interesting truths of parenting. When you trust your kids, your kids feel trusted. When they feel trusted, they make better decisions to keep that trust. When they make better decisions, you trust them more. It's a spiral of positivity.

Admit to yourself and to your boss that you may be missing information. I find it's quite helpful to admit that if you knew more about the situation, you would be less frustrated. This is good because it's honest. Admit it: you don't have all the information. When my sister and I cut the hole in the wall, I misunderstood my dad's anger. I didn't know it at the time, but I didn't have all the information. When we don't have all of the information, we can't fully understand why the other person is feeling what they're feeling.

Simply saying out loud that you do not have all of the information will directly affect how you carry yourself when you approach a challenging conversation. If you think you have it all figured out, that you possess all knowledge, facts, and insight about this situation, what will your posture likely be? My guess is that it will look like this: arrogant, closed, and judgmental. There is no way to engage in a healthy, fruitful conversation if that is your posture.

I first heard this quote in seminary, and I've never forgotten it. It's brilliant. I've found it helps me determine the posture I want to have. Ashley Montagu, a British-American anthropologist, said, "Humans are the only creatures who are able to behave irrationally in the name of reason."[3]

Do you hear what Montagu is saying? What might seem completely irrational to Jenny actually makes sense to me. So who's right? Jenny, of course. I'm not the sharpest knife in the drawer, but I'm not a complete moron either. But what explains the gap between us? We see the world differently. She sees it her way. I see it my way. If I saw it her way, I'm guessing her ideas and suggestions would make more sense to me. And if she saw things my way, I *guarantee* it would make more sense to her.

It does you no good to walk into a situation thinking you have it all figured out. There is always information you're lacking that can help you understand the situation more clearly. And if I repeat that to myself over and over again, it will radically change my posture as I approach a situation. If I saw it your way, I would understand why you feel like you do and why you're doing what you're doing. You need to stop just short of getting that phrase tattooed on your body.

Stay in the balcony to remain emotionally neutral. My professional coach, Dean, has convinced me of this. The drama of a play happens on the stage, not in the balcony. Onstage, the actors in the drama are emotionally engaged as their characters. The more they've taken on the emotions of that character, the better the play will be. In the balcony, you are an observer. You are watching the play, but you are also able to reflect on it from a distance. Those watching in the balcony have the ability to stay emotionally neutral toward the characters, and this allows for more rational and objective thinking.

If you're assuming I'm a cold, dispassionate machine, I should mention that one of my gifts is that I'm a pretty passionate person. My heart is wrapped up in what I do. The danger I face is that when my emotions rise up, I say things I later regret. I can't begin to count the number of meetings I've attended when I've had to apologize for something I've said. It's as if I lose my ability to think clearly and function well when I allow my emotions to lead the way. I'm not alone in this. Fortunately, there's a biological explanation for what happens to me and to those who have this problem.

Have you noticed how difficult it is to remember someone's name when you meet them? Within seconds of a person telling me his name, I've forgotten what he said. I may have even repeated it to myself. "Great to meet you, Garrett." Seconds later, *Wait, what was his name again?* How in the world does that happen? When our emotions rise, our ability to think rationally declines. When we are learning someone's name upon introduction, we are naturally more nervous and anxious because of the social context. When our nervousness rises, our cognitive ability to do something as simple as remembering the word "Garrett" declines. Emotions are such a powerful force for us, which is why we must learn to stay in the balcony when we're in the middle of tense situations.

If you can't stay emotionally neutral about a situation, you're not ready to bring it up. An emotional person is not a stable person, especially in a discussion with their boss. To be able to talk about something potentially complicated and personal, you need to be able to keep your emotions in check. You cannot allow your emotions to lead you to say things you would regret if you hope to maintain influence with others. You need to develop emotional maturity. If you feel you're too angry or upset, just wait. Learn to control those emotions and practice thinking through them by thinking through interactions in advance. Thomas Paine said, "The greatest remedy for anger is delay."[4] Time has this amazing way of calming us down. The further away from a situation we are, the more clear-minded and levelheaded we can be. And the more effective we will be at challenging up. So stay in the balcony as much as possible.

Prepare yourself to be okay with a no. I've never bought a car at a dealership, but I've bought loads of random stuff from Craigslist. Jenny and I have come to an agreement: if she will choose to buy used, I will go and make the purchase. Nothing looks shadier than meeting someone in a Walmart parking lot to negotiate the price of a used dollhouse.

What I've learned from these fascinating interactions is that the person most willing to walk away without the deal usually has the upper hand. On the flipside, the person with the most to lose usually loses. We make worse decisions when we feel like we can't walk away. But "no" is not the end of the world.

When I'm willing to walk away from the conversation with a "no," I handle that challenging conversation better. I put less pressure on others. Most importantly, this says something about what I believe about God. Do I believe God can do what he wants to do if the answer is no? Our good friend and local bar theologian, Garth Brooks, had something profound to say about this in "Unanswered Prayers": "Sometimes God's greatest gifts are unanswered prayers." Sometimes God is giving you an unexpected gift when you get a no to your great, world-changing idea.

I've also learned to translate a no as a *not yet*. If I feel passionate about something, but my boss just doesn't see it the way I see it, I will translate his answer of no into not yet and go back to the drawing board to find a new approach. I refuse to take it as a loss; instead, I choose to see it as a potential approach that didn't work—I can now cross that approach off the list. God is still God. He can find a way. If I believe that he establishes authority and he is not bound by time, I can translate my boss's no into a not yet, and it's not the end of the road. This keeps me energized and allows me to stay in a healthy posture toward the person in authority.

Scott Adams, the voice and author behind the comic strip *Dilbert*, has written a fantastic book called *How to Fail at Almost Everything and Still Win Big*. In talking about careers, Adams writes, "Avoid career traps such as pursuing jobs that require you to sell your limited supply of time while preparing you for nothing better."[5] He says that everything we do should provide preparation for something else we can do in the future. I don't think Scott Adams is a Jesus follower, but what he writes is completely congruent with God's sovereignty and his ability to redeem even our losses. The more you trust God, the healthier your posture will be in those high-stakes, challenging conversations.

The first two ingredients for challenging up, the relationship you have with your boss and your nonphysical, emotional posture, are primarily about you. As we saw in chapter two, identity is the foundation for great leadership. Who you are is more important than what you do and how you do it, but the last two aspects still matter. You are not the only ingredient in all of this. So these last two ingredients drive us to find the meaning behind what we're challenging and the best approach to how we're challenging up.

THE MEANING

Bringing a call for change can be empty if we don't make it very clear why we are bringing this challenge. What's the meaning? The reason behind the challenge? *The Leadership Challenge* says this well: "Leadership is not about challenge for challenge's sake. It's not about shaking things up just to keep people on their toes. It's about challenge with meaning and passion. It's about living life on purpose."[6] I've found this aspect to be a bit complicated for me because I want so badly to make my mark. I want to make a profound difference. I want my life to be useful and purposeful. If you're in professional ministry or working on a church staff, this is especially tricky. One of the main attractions individuals feel toward full time, vocational ministry is the sense of purpose and fulfillment that comes from this work. That's why it's healthy to think through your motives. The temptation is in all of us to make change just for change's sake.

The most powerful reason to challenge the status quo is to *make it better.* Any other reason for change is counterproductive. But not everyone will agree on what defines *better.* The challenge is that it might be clear to you, but it is your responsibility to communicate this and make it crystal clear to your boss. In the first class I took at Dallas Theological Seminary, I'll never forget the legendary professor Dr. Howard Hendricks saying, "If there is a mist in the pulpit, there's fog in the pews." This isn't just true for preaching, though. If you are fuzzy on how a change you propose will make things better, your boss will be confused as well. Make sure the reason for the change and the benefits of the change are clear to you and that you're able to make this clear to others.

Start by finding the why. Begin by answering some simple questions: Why? Why are you suggesting this change? Why will this change make it better? The answer to why is not always easy to find, but if you can nail this, it will help you be clear about the meaning and purpose of this change.

With over thirty million views, Simon Sinek's video has brought insight, and the power of the question of why is no secret anymore. Not only has his TED Talk shaped me, but the guiding principle of his book, *Start with Why: How Great Leaders Inspire Everyone to Take Action*, has been profoundly helpful as well. He writes, "People don't buy what you do; they buy why you do it. And what you do simply proves what you believe."[7] Although pastors and preachers need to be careful not to "peddle the word of God for profit" as the apostle Paul reminds us in 2 Corinthians 2:17, there is a sense in which we are all selling something. When you challenge up, you are selling an idea, a new way, a different path toward a better future. The clearer your *why*, the more they'll buy.

Hold tight to why, but be loose with what. Year after year, our leadership team would bang our heads against the conference table as we evaluated the Sunday of Memorial Day weekend. We were not content with the results we were seeing. Because our suburban churches in the Atlanta area have a lot of families that attend, the school calendar creates our ministry seasons for us. Memorial Day weekend is a clear break between the school-year season and the summer season, and for that reason and many others, it's typically the worst attended Sunday of the year for us.

A few years into this frustrating dilemma, I noticed one of our partner churches had found a simple solution. In all of their communication, they let people know, "We're not meeting on the Sunday of Memorial Day weekend." I remember reading that and thinking, *Well, that fixes the problem. But no church? Can they even do that?* After thinking through all of my theological hoops, I convinced myself that it was okay. And so a few of us bonded together around this idea, and we gently brought it up to the leadership.

Our why was clear: we wanted to begin the summer with as much momentum as possible. Our what was to cancel the Sunday of Memorial Day weekend and apply that energy to the summer. This was our pitch: "Hey, we have an idea. It seems like we are always frustrated and can't find a great solution. What if we use this as an opportunity to kick off the summer as strong as possible and also honor our volunteers who serve so faithfully all year long?"

So, how did it go? Shot down. No chance. No way. Terrible idea. "We can't just cancel church. And, most importantly, do you even love Jesus?" That about summarizes the response we received from the higher-ups. To their credit, they agreed with the why. They also wanted to build as much momentum as possible heading into the summer. But the thought of cancelling a Sunday of services just seemed like too much, at least until we had exhausted every other what. So, year after year, we tinkered and tried multiple options. Because our family ministry directors insist on giving as many volunteers as possible a break for that weekend, we tried having adult services but without children or student ministry environments. That created other problems with the way our adult service felt for those attending for the first time, because there were so many kids in the service. Then we tried to manage our student and children's environments with very few volunteers. Our adult service felt better, but our family ministry leaders were unhappy with the experience of first-time children and students. Either way, every year when we reviewed that weekend, someone was unhappy with the results. Ultimately, nothing feels great when it feels like no one is in attendance. A full room does wonders for everyone. An empty room feels like a sinking ship.

So a few years later, we brought up our suggestion again. What if we didn't hold services for the Sunday of Memorial Day weekend? What if we used the day to give our volunteers a break? What if we took that energy and poured it into the first Sunday of the summer for a big kick-off to a new season? The ideas were the same, but the approach was much different. This time, we brought up the idea earlier in the year, brought a better plan for how to communicate it, positioned it as an opportunity for growth for our churches, and had better answers for the most common objections. We held tightly to the why; we had tried all the options of what; and we were patient but persistent.

After years of conversation and debate, the leadership decided to pull the trigger and give it a shot. We think it has worked. Our attendance in the summer has been stronger, our volunteers have felt appreciated, and I'll let you guess how the decision affected our staff culture. Finding the *meaning* behind the change empowered us to present a challenging idea. It also helped that we worked hard to make it less personal and to give a compelling answer to the questions of why and how.

YOUR APPROACH

Working for a great leader has many benefits. My favorite aspect of working for Andy Stanley is that I feel like I'm getting a graduate-level leadership degree just by observation and osmosis. Every leader has their greatest hits of leadership maxims, those phrases and sayings that come up time and time again. As for Andy, what I have learned from him on *approach* is definitely on my "Best of" list for him.

We have all had conversations derailed because of a poor approach. The way you lead into a conversation can often trump the content of the conversation. We have all been in conversations where we were right, but we ended up apologizing because we had the wrong approach. When I was first married, my desire to be right would cause me to bring more energy and passion to conversations. I remember being at a restaurant with Jenny. There was something wrong with the food. I was clearly right, but the tone I used in speaking with the server about the issue really bothered Jenny. I was right in sending the food back, but before I could be on the same page as Jenny, I needed to apologize to the server because of how I approached the situation. Approach is everything. With the right approach, you can say just about anything. With the wrong approach, it doesn't matter if you're right or wrong; it won't work.

Adjust your approach to fit the person. In order to know what approach to take, we need to be deeply acquainted with our boss's wiring, temperament, and personality. Great spouses study each other to have a great marriage; you need to study your boss in the same way. There's a lot you can do to get to know your boss's style without taking it too far. Our kids crack up every time at that line in *Planes: Fire and Rescue* when Lil' Dipper whispers to Dusty, "I like watching you sleep." I wouldn't suggest stalking your boss, but landing somewhere just short of that is a great idea.

What is your boss's personality type?

Does your boss think concretely or abstractly?

What level of detail does your boss need?

How does your boss like to receive information?

Do you need to send an email ahead of time with all the details, or should you follow up with an email after the conversation?

These are all questions you can ask your boss when emotions are low. Later, in challenging conversations, if you have done your homework, it will show. The bottom line is that you do some homework and learn the approach that best fits your boss.

Declare your intentions before you challenge. Every great wedding gives the bride and groom a chance to declare their intentions. This is where they publicly say what the wedding is all about, and I really appreciate that. You don't spend all that money, invite all those people, and waste all of our time by not making it clear *why* we are all there. And the same is true when you need to have a difficult conversation. Declare your intentions up-front. It's like clipping a carabiner to a harness. If something goes awry, your declared intentions provide a safety net in a free-falling conversation. Here are a few examples:

- "I really believe in you and I love working for you. I have something I want to bring up that could help us grow. Maybe I'm missing something, but I think this might be a better solution for all of us."
- "I think I've identified something that is holding us back and if I were in your shoes, I would want to know what it is. I think I have an idea about how to solve it. Would you mind if I shared that with you?"
- "I want your advice on something. I have an idea I think

will make us better, but I want to know what you think about it. I've thought a lot about it. It might initially create some complications, but in the end, I think we'll be glad we made the change because of the results it could produce."

How you start out and what you say are so crucial. Before you get in anyone's space, trying to throw around your brilliant ideas that have the potential to wreck someone else's world, lead with a clear statement of your intentions. You'll either be glad you did or regret that you didn't.

Ask questions of curiosity and mean it. One of the constant pieces of feedback I receive about my leadership is that I have a tendency to move too quickly. When I'm moving quickly for the sake of progress, I have the tendency to jump to conclusions that may or may not be true. When I misjudge someone, it negatively affects the relationship. No one likes feeling judged, even when it's spot-on. Feeling incorrectly judged feels wrong on multiple levels.

Disciplining myself to lead with questions helps me avoid the trap of rash judgments. Curious questions cause humility. Lately, I've begun every important conversation similar to this: "I've got a lot of thoughts about this situation, but I know you do as well. Tell me how you're processing it." This is crucial for me. Incorrect assumptions create walls and cause humiliation. If you choose to start the challenging conversation with questions, it will teach you something. It will build trust, and it will save you some embarrassment.

MORE THAN A FEELING

The band Boston says there are moments that are more than a feeling. I would agree with them, but barely. You are more than a feeling, but your feelings have a pretty substantial role in your life. They matter deeply. Let me try to explain.

Every once in a while, my pocket computer (also known as my smartphone) does the most unusual thing. It rings. Who calls anyone these days? And please, for the love, do not leave me a voicemail. Just text me. Or email me. But do not leave me a voicemail. I return voicemails like Charles Barkley swings a golf club. It's bad.

When your phone rings and you see the name of a person pop up, what happens? Well, it depends on how you feel. And how you feel is determined by the name you see. In that moment, the person is a feeling to you, and nothing more than a feeling. Sorry, Boston. Now, if that happens when your phone rings, guess what? It also happens when your name pops up when you call your boss. Your boss sees your name and you become a feeling to your boss. So here's the seventy-dollar question: how does your boss feel about you when your name pops up on his or her phone?

How you challenge will determine how your boss feels about you. Obviously, we want our boss to get all the positive feels when they think of us. Why? Clearly, so they'll pay us more. Ha! Just kidding. Well, sort of. If you really want to lead when you're not in charge, you want your boss to feel positive vibes about you for the sake of influence. Nothing is more miserable than being in a job where you have no influence. And nothing is more exhilarating than the opportunity to make change, to make something better, and to be able to expand your influence. A good paycheck is great. A job with influence and opportunity is even better. So learn to challenge up well. There's far more at stake than you realize.

CHAPTER 10

YOUR NEXT
CHAPTER STARTS
TODAY

You've made it to the final chapter. Congratulations. I honestly didn't think you would read this far, but I'm glad you did. I want you to imagine yourself five years from now. You're the boss. You have that corner office with the great view, a big desk, and a globe in the corner (I don't know why the globe is there, but it seems like something an important person might keep in their office). You have worked your way up the ladder at the business/church/organization you currently work for, and now you are running the show. You're the one in charge. Now what?

This is a situation I imagined nearly every day when I was in my twenties. I loved to picture myself with my feet up on my desk, looking out over the Atlanta skyline as people reported in to me. There were times when I thought, *If only I was in charge . . .* or *Once I'm the boss I am going to . . .* It was only too natural for me to think about how I would manage things once I was given the authority I needed. Sadly, I was so focused on what I would do in the future that I missed opportunities to grow as a leader right then and there. My perspective was toward an idealistic dream, but I didn't have a clear plan for how to get there. Now there is nothing wrong with thinking and planning ahead. But there is a danger in focusing too much on what we want to change or what we'll do when we're in charge, *and instead, failing to start doing anything right now.* Inevitably, we miss out on the possibility of developing as leaders before we ever get to be in charge.

Great leaders know how to lead when they're in charge because they've been leading long before they were ever given that authority. That's the big idea I hope you take away from this book. I hope you see that it's possible to lead from where you are right now. I hope you know you don't have to wait for that future position you've been dreaming about to begin leading. Leadership starts right now, wherever you are.

One of the best things you can do today is to begin asking yourself questions about how and why you want to lead when you're in charge. Then start leading with those answers in mind. Anyone can daydream about what they will do once they're in charge. But it takes a unique person, a real leader, to imagine this reality and then put it into action before they have that position of authority. I have read enough books on leadership to know that if you close this book and don't act on any of the things you just read, then you have wasted your time. I don't want that to happen. That's why the steps I've shared for leading when you're not in charge are actionable and applicable to anyone. In this last chapter, we are going to answer several questions. My hope is that as you begin to answer questions about how you want to lead, you'll see that you can begin to lead from right where you are today. There is no magic formula to leading when you're not in charge. If you were waiting for a big, secret reveal in the last chapter, I'm sorry to let you down.

The truth is, all we need is a perspective shift. When we

stop thinking about how we want to lead in the future and start looking for opportunities to lead right now, we truly learn how to make ourselves, and those around us, better. Real leadership isn't about having the authority to lead. Authority matters, but it's a tool that makes good leadership effective, not the secret sauce that makes everything about leadership suddenly happen. Instead, we need to learn how to cultivate influence. And that's something all of us can do. Each one of us is called to be a leader in some capacity—in our jobs, our schools, our churches, our communities, and our cities. These organizations are waiting for people like you to step up and lead.

REGARDING YOUR REPUTATION

One of the most important questions you can ask yourself is this: what do you want people to say about you when you are finally in charge? If you're like me, you've pictured yourself as the boss plenty of times. But have you ever imagined what your reputation will be as a boss? These questions matter for a couple of reasons. First, they force you to think about the impact of your leadership on other people. It's easy to daydream about looking down on others, but it's more challenging when you seriously contemplate others looking up to you. Second, once you answer these questions about how you want your future self to be, you can start working to become that person today.

When I was young, I was so busy judging the reputations of those in charge that I rarely thought about my own reputation. I naively thought that once I was in a position of power, I would garner a reputation as a leader. Ask any leader and they will tell you that's just not true. Having a title doesn't give you a reputation as a great leader. I love how Dave Ramsey put this in *EntreLeadership*: "I confused having a *position* with real leadership. Having children doesn't make you a good parent; it means you had sex. That's all."[1]

Nothing magically changes about your reputation when you are placed in a position of authority. The same reputation you have without power stays with you when you do have power and authority. Great leaders look ahead to the future and begin to act today to become who they want to be. In fact, the whole purpose of this book is to encourage you to begin leading from where you are. Don't wait until you are in charge to be the leader you want to be. Chances are, *if you wait to start leading, you will never be put in a position to lead anyway.* Start asking yourself what type of leader you want to be tomorrow. And start becoming that type of leader today. Because whether you realize it or not, you are building a reputation for yourself, both as a leader and as a person.

> Start asking yourself what type of leader you want to be tomorrow. And start becoming that type of leader today.

Your reputation matters. But like everything that matters in life, it isn't something you start to work on tomorrow. It isn't formed overnight. You're forming a reputation right now, whether you're in charge or not.

THE TOTAL TOTEM POLE

Think back to the last time you had a job at the very bottom of a company. Maybe you were an intern or in an entry-level role, but either way, you were in a position with zero authority. How did you view your boss? And not just your immediate boss, but the person at the very top. You probably didn't know him or her on a first-name basis, so what was the reputation of the person in charge at the very top?

Fast-forward five years. You are that person now. Think about how people might view you at the top. What will your reputation be with the person at the very bottom of the totem pole? Good managers lead with their entire staff in mind. From upper and mid-level managers, all the way down to interns and janitors. The people at the top may never interact with the people at the bottom, but that doesn't mean they don't have influence there. In fact, the relationship between the person at the very top and the person at the very bottom of an organization tells you a lot about someone's leadership ability. Good leaders are viewed favorably by those closest to them in the company. Great leaders are viewed favorably by everyone in the company.

Jesus knew this. In John 4, Jesus has an interaction with a Samaritan woman. In that culture, there was no one lower on the totem pole than a Samaritan woman. For starters, Jews looked down on Samaritans. They were a second-rate culture. In addition to that, women had practically no standing in society. So this woman was the least important person in the society of the least important culture. To everyone around her, she was a nobody. But to Jesus, she was a human being created in the image of God, someone deserving dignity and respect. That Jesus would even address her at all was already a step outside the societal norms. That he would treat her with respect was simply unheard of. But this was how Jesus led. He didn't consult with the disciples. He didn't try to build a great reputation among the people of power. He focused on talking to everyone and treating even the most marginalized within society with respect.

The Samaritan woman was not an outlier either. Jesus had countless interactions with tax collectors, prostitutes, and lepers. He talked to anyone society considered worthless. And in each of these instances, he spoke with respect and did wonders for his reputation. That's our job as leaders. We must lead with the total totem pole in mind, regardless of our own position on the pole. If you are at the bottom of the corporate ladder right now, start leading in a way that people in every position can respect. And as you rise through the organization, lead with the person at the bottom in mind. That's what Jesus did. You can tell the character of a leader not by how they are treated by their equals, but by how they are viewed by those under them.

PEOPLE LEAVE MANAGERS, NOT JOBS

People's opinions of you are not going to drastically change once you're in charge. Just because people respect your position of authority does not necessarily mean they will respect you. Suddenly gaining authority will not have the power to reverse or improve your reputation. If the people you work with didn't respect you before you held a position of power, then the respect you may or may not receive at the top will be superficial. It's important to understand and manage the influence you have now so you know what to do on that day when you finally get the promotion you've been hoping for. Otherwise, you might end up being the boss people hate working for. Don't believe that's possible? Consider this. A Gallup study showed that fifty percent of people who leave their jobs do so because of their bosses.[2]

Fifty percent. If two people have left under your employment, odds are one of them left because of you. Yikes. How many leaders think to take responsibility for someone leaving?

The quality of any individual's job will be determined by three key variables:

- What you do
- Whom you do it with
- How much money you make

Or, to put it another way, it all comes down to the what, the who, and the "dolla bills, y'all." If the who (the coworkers and the boss) are not enjoyable, then either the work or the pay has to be great. I would argue that if we were to rank these three things in order of importance, the who would be at the very top of the list. If you've ever worked a job you hate with people you love, then you know exactly what I'm talking about. Being surrounded by great people can make doing even menial tasks enjoyable. Just look at Jim and Pam from *The Office*. Both of them seemed to stick it out in a less than desirable office culture because they had each other. Even a well paying job can be pretty miserable if the people or the work isn't enjoyable.

MAKING YOUR SUCCESS OUR SUCCESS

As a leader, it is your responsibility to create an environment where people enjoy their work and find meaning in it. You also need to create a team environment where others enjoy working with you. If people enjoy working *with* you, it is much more likely they will potentially enjoy working *for* you. What kind of working relationships do you want to cultivate? Those where your success is seen as success for those you work with. Solomon says, "When the righteous thrive, the people rejoice; when the wicked rule, the people groan" (Prov. 29:2).

Do others celebrate your success? Are your coworkers happy when you thrive in your work? If the answer to both of these questions is yes, then keep doing exactly what you're doing. If the answer is no or you aren't sure, think about what you need to change in order to be a leader worth cheering for. This matters now, because it will matter later.

The best way to be the type of leader people want to celebrate is to care deeply about the people you work with. Effective leaders are inclusive. When they succeed, the people around them succeed. A *rising tide lifts all boats*. They create environments where people at every level of the company want to work hard because they know everyone benefits when everyone is working at full potential. Inclusive leaders do not isolate themselves as authoritarian figures. Rather, they include themselves in the discussion as influential innovators. These leaders know the best thing they can do for themselves is to push those around them to be their best. These are the types of leaders people celebrate. Why? Because they feel like they are a part of that person's success.

Again, let's take a look at Jesus. There is no disputing that he was the leader of his disciples. Clearly, he was the guy in charge. But did Jesus keep the disciples around so they could serve him and do the jobs he didn't want to do? No. He surrounded himself with disciples so he could teach and train them. He was preparing them to carry on the momentum of his ministry. He was entrusting them with his mission. So he leveraged his power, like a counterweight, to build others up. In Matthew 10, Jesus sends the disciples into towns and villages to heal the sick and spread the gospel. But he didn't just send them out and hope for the best. No, he equipped them. He told the disciples where to go, what to say, what to do, and even what to take (vv. 6–10). He also spent time encouraging them and warning them about the job ahead of them. That's leadership.

Obviously, Jesus could have done everything he told the disciples to do himself. He did not give them tasks he was incapable of doing, nor was he being lazy by micromanaging. He was forcing them to live up to their potential. That's what we are called to do as leaders, and that's something we can do whether we are in charge or not. It's not saying, "What can you do to make me look better?" It's saying, "What can I do to make you be better?" Jesus didn't use his authority to boss the disciples around. He used his influence to make them reach their fullest potential. It's this type of leadership that people are eager to work under. Leaders who focus solely on their own success are everywhere. And leaders who focus on the success of those under them are rare.

Are you the type of leader that makes others better? When people watch the way you lead, do they want to be like you or do they want to be as different from you as possible? Because not only do leaders make those around them better, they live and lead in a way that's worth emulating.

MAKE A LEADERSHIP LIST

One of the best things you can do to be a better leader is to watch and learn from the people who are in charge. Great leaders have the ability to learn from those above them and apply those lessons. Look at leaders you admire (and leaders you don't admire) and start paying attention to how they lead. The best leaders are learners. They realize there is always something to learn from the people around them. When I worked in entry-level positions at our church, I constantly watched the person at the top, because I wanted to know if he was using what he was selling. Did he actually believe what he was teaching?

No matter what job you have, or what type of boss you have, you can learn how to lead, and how *not* to lead. You can learn just as much from a terrible boss as you can from a great one. Pay attention. Take notes on what you like and don't like. Here's an example of a list I made when I was in my twenties. These are some notes I wrote down as I was watching figures of authority and how they led.

Dos:

- Value every opinion, especially those that contradict your own.
- Tell people you value the work they are putting in.
- Lead by action first and word second.
- Express expectations and make sure those around you know what you want and need from them.
- Provide as much encouragement and affirmation as possible.
- Be efficient with tasks and effective with people.

Don'ts:

- Underestimate the intern.
- Ignore an idea/belief/criticism shared by more than one person.

- Take the people who are doing the dirty work for granted.
- Schedule meetings that have no clear goal or purpose.
- Act as if you're better than everyone, even if you are.
- Undervalue the time others are putting in to make your job easier.

As you are making your list, be aware that others may be watching you and making their own lists of dos and don'ts. If the people around you are smart, they are learning just as much from you as you are from them. Where does your leadership style fall on this list? Do people look at you for how they should or shouldn't behave? Is the way you lead, whether you're in charge or not, worth emulating? If you aren't setting an example worth following now, it's unlikely anything will change once you're in charge.

YOUR PLACE IN LINE

Ultimately, the best leader we can emulate is Jesus. He was the best leader to ever live and not because he had all the power. He did, but he relinquished those rights and claims to become a willing servant to God's mission to redeem and save us. As the Son of God, the second person of the Trinity, Jesus had an eternal claim to more authority than anyone that has ever lived. He could have wielded this authority and power, threatening to smite anyone who stood in his way. But he didn't. He never used his authority to force anyone to comply with his will. He used influence and self-sacrifice. Earlier, we looked at this passage from Philippians. Let's look one more time as a reminder of the kind of leadership we are called to exercise.

In your relationships with one another, have the same mindset as Christ Jesus:

> Who, being in very nature God,
>> did not consider equality with God something to be used
>>> to his own advantage;
>> rather, he made himself nothing
>>> by taking the very nature of a servant.

PHIL. 2:5–7

If Jesus didn't consider equality with God a thing to be used
to his advantage, then why should we think we can throw around
our authority to get what we want? What do you want to be? A
lead pastor, a CEO, maybe the President of the United States?
What do all of these positions have in common? They have zero
authority compared to Jesus. But here's the thing: it wasn't the
authority Jesus possessed that made him a great leader. It was
his influence over the minds and hearts of people, influence
cultivated by speaking truth and challenging the status quo, by
serving others, by healing people and meeting their needs. It
was an influence cultivated by giving people hope and vision
for the future. Ultimately, it was influence earned by demon-
strating the depth of his love for people, by sacrificing himself
on their behalf. That's leadership. And it's our job to emulate
his example. The question we should ask ourselves is this: are
the people I'm leading here for me or am I here for them? Great
leaders sacrifice themselves for the good of others. Jesus laid his
life down. If the Son of God didn't lead with self-service as his
priority, then neither should we. Jesus teaches us that leadership
isn't about being served. It's about serving. And the best part
about serving is that anyone can do it. Anyone, no matter his or

her position, can serve others. From the lead pastor or CEO to the summer intern, we all share the responsibility of service and the obligation to love our neighbors as we love ourselves.

NOW WHAT?

There are four words that rattle around in my brain on a regular basis. These four words create accountability for how I'm living each day. They create urgency for my beliefs, helping me to make sure they are evident in my actions. If my stated beliefs aren't showing up in my everyday life, then they're just statements and claims. I'm not actually living by faith. So these four words give gravity to what I'm doing right now, not just what I *say* I believe.

"As now, so then."

Or to put these four words into our context: as you're leading now, so you will lead then. If you aren't leading through influence now, you won't lead through influence then. If you are waiting on authority to begin to have influence, you'll be forced to depend on that authority when you're in charge. You have to start now. *As now, so then.*

My point in writing this book was to help you see that you can be the leader you want to be today. You have everything you need to lead. You have the examples of those around you. You have the example of Jesus. You interact with people you can serve every day. Leadership is not about waiting until people call you a leader. It's about doing everything you can to lead right where you are.

I've tried to give you some practical advice, which I hope you can begin to apply. But if there is one thing everyone needs to do, no matter his or her position of authority, it's this—*love*. Love is commonly overlooked when people talk about leadership. Great leaders love *what* they do, who they do it *with*, and who they do it *for*. Jesus said, "By this everyone will know that you are my disciples, if you love one another" (John 13:35).

That's what Jesus did. He was the best leader to ever walk the face of the earth. He began a movement that has lasted over two thousand years. And how did he do it? By loving each and every person he came into contact with. There are a lot of things Jesus did that you and I can't do (like walking on water, feeding five thousand people with a few loaves of bread and some fish, raising someone from the dead). But loving other people is something anyone can do. Not only that, it's something great leaders do well. I'll never forget hearing Patrick Lencioni say this at Willow Creek's Leadership Summit: "Management is good ministry. We are called to love the people we lead." Sound familiar?

The mission of our church is to lead people into a growing relationship with Jesus. With so many issues and challenges facing people today, I believe Jesus is the answer. That's not trite and that's not lip service. Jenny and I have leveraged all of our lives to this end. Why, then, have I written this book on leadership? The longer I've served as a pastor, the more convinced I am that the church needs better leaders. And not just as a formal organization with staff and pastors, but throughout the entire church. We need followers of Christ who are living out their faith as leaders in all of their diverse and wonderful callings—as teachers, parents, accountants, lawyers, musicians, artists, coaches, janitors, auto mechanics, plumbers—you name it! If Jesus is the hope of the world, then the church, the people of Jesus, is the vehicle for that hope. And if you are a pastor or teacher in the church, your people need to hear from you what it means to be a godly leader. They need to hear the call to step up and lead, even if they aren't in positions of authority.

I'm done treading water, just waiting on authority or a title to start leading. I'm determined to lead like life depends on it, because I believe it does. I'm not going to buy the lie that says I need more authority to have more influence. If the way of influence really outpaces the way of authority, let's get on the road together and start moving ahead. Great leadership depends on influence. The more influence you cultivate today, the more you'll have tomorrow.

Choose to start leading today, whether you're in charge or not.

It starts right now.

Chapter 1: The Oddity of Leadership

1. Sinek, Simon. "Why Good Leaders Make You Feel Safe." https://www.ted.com/talks/simon_sinek_why_good_leaders _make_you_feel_safe.
2. Collins, Jim. "Good to Great." FastCompany.com, https://www. fastcompany.com/43811/good-great.
3. Tabrizi, Benham. "The Key to Change is Middle Management." *Harvard Business Review.* https://hbr.org/2014/10/ the-key-to-change-is-middle-management.

Chapter 2: Identity Crisis

1. Zucker, Jerry. *First Knight.* DVD. Los Angeles: Columbia Pictures, 1995.
2. Morel, Pierre. *Taken.* DVD. Los Angeles: 20th Century Fox, 2008.

Chapter 3: Reclaim Kibosh

1. *Seinfeld.* "The Opera." Episode 49. Directed by Tom Cherones. Written by Larry Charles. NBC, November 4, 1992.
2. In Jewish hermeneutics, there are four basic interpretive categories: literal (*peshat*), philosophical (*remez*), inferred (*derash*), and mystical (*sod*). The first letter of each one of those Hebrew words is used to create the acronym PRDS, more commonly referred to and pronounced by my Rabbi friends as "pardes." This is still used as the framework for Jewish exegesis and interpretative study of the Torah. A Jewish Rabbi would consider this connection between *kabash* and *kibosh* to be a *remez*, not a *peshat*. It's philosophical, not literal. Even though we cannot find

a literal connection between *kabash* and *kibosh*, it's accurate to say that these two words make the exact sound, yet have two distinct and contrary definitions. To use the wordplay to make a point is a normal and acceptable form of Jewish hermeneutics. To the Hebrew people, the word, *kabash*, must have meant something beautiful. Today, when someone uses that same sound, *kibosh*, they mean something completely different. No one knows how we got here, but no one can deny the distortion of where we are.

Chapter 4: Lead Yourself

1. Ballard, Glenn and Siedah Garrett. *Man in the Mirror.* Los Angeles: Epic Records, 1988.
2. Maxwell, John. *Leadership Handbook: 26 Critical Lessons Every Leader Needs* (Nashville: Thomas Nelson, 2015), 17.
3. Watkins, Michael D. *The First 90 Days: Proven Strategies for Getting Up to Speed Faster and Smarter* (Boston: Harvard Business Review Press, 2013), 20.
4. Collins, Jim. *How the Mighty Fall: And Why Some Companies Never Give In* (New York: HarperCollins, 2011), 4.
5. Patterson, Kerry, Joseph Grenny, Ron McMillian, and Al Switzler. *Crucial Conversations: Tools for Talking When the Stakes are High* (New York: McGraw-Hill, 2002).
6. Stone, Douglas, Bruce Patton, and Sheila Heen. *Difficult Conversations: How to Discuss What Matters Most* (London: Penguin Books, 2010).

Chapter 5: Choose Positivity

1. Covey, Stephen, R. *Seven Habits of Highly Successful People* (Free Press: New York, 1989), 28.
2. Ibid, 17.
3. Dale Carnegie Training. "What Drives Employee Engagement and Why It Matters," p. 6. https://www.dalecarnegie.com/assets/1/7/driveengagement_101612_wp.pdf.
4. Ibid.

5. Lencioni, Patrick. *The Advantage: Why Organizational Health Trumps Everything Else in Business* (San Francisco: Jossey-Bass, 2012), 47.

6. Camalier, Greg. *Muscle Shoals*. Netflix. Dallas: Magnolia Films, 2013.

Chapter 6: Think Critically

1. Cowherd, Colin, *You Herd Me: I'll Say It If Nobody Else Will* (London: Penguin Press, 2013), 28.

2. http://www.usatoday.com/story/gameon/2012/10/24/rodgers-professor-never-succeed/1654723/.

3. McChesney, Chris, Sean Covey, and Jim Huling. *The 4 Disciplines of Execution: Achieving Your Wildly Important Goals* (New York: Free Press, 2012), 30.

4. http://www1.hansgrohe.com/assets/at—de/1404_Hansgrohe_Select_ConsumerSurvey_EN.pdf.

5. Walvoord, John F. and Roy B. Zuck. *The Bible Knowledge Commentary*. Logos Bible Software (Colorado Springs: David C. Cook, 2002).

Chapter 7: Reject Passivity

1. Hylton, Jeremy. "The Merry Wives of Windsor." Tech.MIT.edu. http://shakespeare.mit.edu/merry_wives/merry_wives.2.2.html.

2. Turner, Bonnie, Terry Turner, and Fred Wolf. *Tommy Boy*. DVD. Directed by Peter Segal. Los Angeles: Paramount Pictures, 1995.

Chapter 8: Challenging Up

1. Kouzes, James M. and Barry Z. Posner. *The Leadership Challenge, 3rd ed.* (San Francisco: Jossey-Bass, 2003), 180.

2. Associated Press. "Brewers Jonathan Lucroy Rejects Trade to the Indians." *New York Times*. July 31, 2016. https://mobile.nytimes.com/2016/08/01/sports/baseball/milwaukee-brewers-jonathan-lucroy-cleveland-indians.html.

3. *Seinfeld.* "The Strongbox." Episode 170. Directed by Andy Ackerman. Written by Dan O'Keefe and Billy Kimball. NBC, February 5, 1998.

4. Barra, Alan. "How Curt Flood Changed Baseball and Killed His Career in the Process." *The Atlantic.* July 12, 2011. https://www .theatlantic.com/entertainment/archive/2011/07/how-curt-flood -changed-baseball-and-killed-his-career-in-the-process/241783/.

5. Kouzes, James M. and Barry Z. Posner. *The Leadership Challenge, 4th ed* (San Francisco: Jossey-Bass, 2008), 48.

6. Widener, Chris. *Leadership Rules: How to Become the Leader You Want to Be* (San Francisco: Jossey-Bass, 2010), 156.

Chapter 9: Breaking Down Challenging Up

1. Cuddy, Amy. "Your Body Language Shapes Who You Are." YouTube, October 1, 2012. https://www.youtube.com/ watch?v=Ks-_Mh1QhMc.

2. Buckingham, Marcus. *The One Thing You Need to Know.* (New York: Free Press, 2005), 22.

3. Quote of the Day. http://www.qotd.org/search/single. html?qid=2016.

4. AZ Quotes. http://www.azquotes.com/quote/223506.

5. Adams, Scott. *How to Fail at Almost Everything and Still Win Big: Kind of the Story of My Life* (New York: Portfolio Publishing, 2013), 230.

6. Kouzes, James M. and Barry Z. Posner. *The Leadership Challenge, 3rd ed* (San Francisco: Jossey-Bass, 2003), 184.

7. Sinek, Simon. "Start with Why." YouTube, September 29, 2013. https://www.youtube.com/watch?v=sioZd3AxmnE.

Chapter 10: Your Next Chapter Starts Today

1. Ramsey, Dave. *EntreLeadership: 20 Years of Practical Business Wisdom from the Trenches* (New York: Howard Books, 2011), 15.

2. Snyder, Benjamin. "Half of us Quit our Job Because of a Bad Boss." *Fortune.* http://fortune.com/2015/04/02/quit-reasons/.

New Video Study for Your Team or Small Group

If you've enjoyed this book, now you can go deeper with the companion video study!

In this six-session study, Clay Scroggins helps you apply the principles in *How to Lead When You're Not in Charge* to your life. The study guide includes video notes, group discussion questions, and personal study and reflection materials for in-between sessions.

Study Guide
9780310095934

DVD
9780310095958

Available now at your favorite bookstore,
or streaming video on StudyGateway.com.

I'll let you in on a leadership secret: people don't follow titles. They follow courage and integrity. That means true leaders become people of influence, regardless of their spot on an organizational chart. If you're ready to lead right where you are, Clay Scroggins understands—and *How to Lead When You're Not in Charge* can show you how to start.

DAVE RAMSEY, BESTSELLING AUTHOR AND
NATIONALLY SYNDICATED RADIO SHOW HOST

Clay's approach is authentic, fun, and engaging. With experience and practical examples, Clay reminds us that our influence is not tied to our titles. Regardless of your industry, if you are in an entry-level or C-level job, this book will become a must-read for you and your team.

JEREMY WALLS, SVP, CHIEF MARKETING
OFFICER, MIAMI DOLPHINS